WHISPERS FROM WARWICK 2

MORE MYSTERY FROM A MEDIEVAL TOWN

To Angela

Steve

Best wishes.

Steve Garrison Dip.Para.Psychol

Contents

For my three sons and four grandchildren
who have made my life complete.

INTRODUCTION

It is said that everyone has a ghost story. It might be from the school playground or perhaps that time when an old clock that hadn't worked for years suddenly started chiming on the day of a relative's funeral. It might not even be your story, but merely an urban myth that stopped you from driving down a local deserted lane or possibly prevented you walking past a particular old house. That house with the overgrown garden that you always quicken your pace past, the hair on your neck standing up as you imagine eyes staring at you from behind closed curtains.

The idea of the dead remaining on Earth in spirit has long been a popular trope in literature, the notion featuring in texts as renowned as the Bible and Shakespeare's Macbeth. Outside of books, ghost sightings have been reported by people from all walks of life, every degree of intelligence and literacy and in every country in the world. In the UK, the prestigious Universities of Oxford and Cambridge even formed their own societies dedicated to investigating ghosts and hauntings. Perhaps the most notable of these societies was the 'Ghost Club' founded in 1862. It is believed to be the oldest such organisation in the world and includes amongst its membership Sir Arthur Conan Doyle and Charles Dickens.

People may believe in ghosts for lots of reasons, such as the comfort it brings to consider that lost loved ones are with us in our time of need. If they are a 'mental aberration' as some have claimed, then the aberration is common to a very large number of people. Just as puzzling as the idea of accepting that ghosts exist is the question as to why particular places acquire a reputation for being haunted, regardless of whether they are historic or modern. And why should people who have absolutely no connection with one another and may visit a place week, months and even years apart have the same uncanny experience.

Back in 1950 when the American pollster Gallup asked Britons whether they believed in ghosts, about one in ten admitted they did. When the same question was posed in the 1970s the figure had more than doubled to one in five and by the early 1990s it was just under one in three. When asked by Gallup in 2005, 37 per cent of respondents claimed they thought houses could be haunted. Professor Richard Wiseman, a leading psychologist and paranormal investigator at the University of Hertfordshire, estimates that a quarter of British adults (around 15 million people) claim to have experienced a ghost sighting or some kind of paranormal activity. A study published in early 2023 claimed that 52 per cent of Brits' have some kind of paranormal beliefs. My own research in Warwick has shown that many people are not seeking any kind of scientific explanation for their experiences. They are content with what they believe. Their ghosts belong to them.

Personally, I would suggest that leaving yourself open to a little spookiness is harmless. It is a curiously optimistic and wishful way of looking at the world. Whilst researching my previous book 'Whispers from Warwick' I was astonished by the number of hauntings and paranormal occurrences reported to me by local people. I started my investigations with an open and perhaps even cynical mind, but by the time the book was completed I found myself even more curious and convinced that there must be so much more to be discovered from the inhabitants of this extraordinary town. So, it has been the case, I was both surprised and delighted by the enthusiasm for 'Whispers from Warwick' from locals and visitors to the town alike. Consequently, many more people have offered up their own personal stories to me. Other conversations I've had with like-minded enthusiasts for both the town and the supernatural have uncovered tales and folklore that I had previously been unaware of. I'm thrilled to be able to share even more tales of mystery, hauntings, and strangeness from Warwick.

So, the next time you find yourself in the town, look around you. Try touching the stone foundations or running your fingers along the cold masonry of one of the many historic buildings. Ponder the lives that have passed through those stones and whether any memories of them have been recorded within. Just maybe, if you're there at the right moment, those memories will reveal themselves to you. I hope you will find my latest stories as intriguing and compelling as I do.

"

All houses where men have lived and died
Are haunted houses. Through the open doors
The harmless phantoms on their errands glide,
With feet that make no sound upon the floors
We meet them at the door-way, on the stair,
Along the passages they come and go,
Impalpable impressions in the air,
A sense of something moving to and fro.
There are more guests at table than the hosts
Invited; the illuminated hall
Is thronged with quiet, inoffensive ghosts,
As silent as the pictures on the wall.

From 'Haunted Houses' by Henry Wadsworth Longfellow

THE MEDIUM

I have been very fortunate to meet a great number of interesting and entertaining individuals during my explorations into the unexplained of Warwick. Taking the time to sit and really listen to the genuine stories that people have been so eager to share is an aspect of my research that I find particularly gratifying.

Shortly after retiring I took on a part time summer job with the town council, as one of several rather grandly titled – 'Town Ambassadors'. During the peak tourist season, the town ambassadors provide a service meeting and greeting visitors, in effect providing a mobile tourist information service. In my first book, 'Whispers from Warwick' I briefly outlined my history and love for the town, and I enjoyed the role of town ambassador very much, especially on those days when the sun was shining. With great respect for time and stories that people had given me during the research for my first book, I very much wanted it to remain a platform to share those stories, keeping myself in the background as much as possible. This second book provides me with an opportunity to share a personal and peculiar encounter that I experienced whilst writing 'Whispers from Warwick', an encounter that in many ways, spurred me on to complete and publish it.

In the Summer of 2022, after a very busy morning assisting, guiding, and chatting with excited visitors to the town, I was taking a chance to rest and sat eating my lunch in the beautiful sunshine bathed gardens adjacent to St Marys church. A smiling lady approached from the archways into the gardens. I was wearing a town council issued, and it must be noted, particularly bright and garish orange polo shirt with the words 'Town Ambassador' emblazoned across it in large letters. I naturally assumed she was about to ask for advice or directions having spent the morning doing exactly that. Rather than engaging me with such a question however, she paused awkwardly for half a minute or so before asking "Can I ask what it is you're writing about the town?".

This took me aback, not least because I had a sandwich, rather than a pen and paper in my hand at the time. I was indeed some way into writing 'Whispers from Warwick' and, although entirely possible given the number of faces I was seeing daily, I was sure that I had never met this lady. I naturally assumed she must have gleaned some knowledge of my venture and somehow recognised me. Confirming that I was writing a book, she sat while I gave her a brief overview of what it was about before curiously asking her how she had come to know of my endeavour. I was caught off guard for a second time however as she claimed her 'intuition' had told her so and she was a practising medium. Despite my acknowledged interests in the weird and unexplained, where mediumship is concerned, I have long been in possession of a healthy dose of cynicism and was more cynical at the time of my encounter than I perhaps am now. With the sun shining and her having a quiet but intense demeanour, rather than churlishly challenge the lady on her claim, I was happy to indulge her further. In both hope and expectation, I inwardly thought that she might have a ghost story of her own to share with me. The conversation that followed still completely fascinates me.

The lady at some point finally introduced herself to me as Estelle, and sat, what for me, was uncomfortably close after the preceding pandemic years. I eased myself as far as I could to the end of the seat, but she shuffled with me, fixing me with pale bright blue eyes and ultimately making me feel quite anxious. In 1970 she had been 16 years old when she had her first spiritual experience in her family's 17th Century home in central Warwick. The experience she said, has had a profound effect on her life ever since. Estelle claimed that it led her to developing the gift of 'automatic writing' and into a life affected by the supernatural, the paranormal and the bizarre.

The explanation of what 'automatic writing' represents is varied depending on spiritual or religious interpretation. However, I'm comfortable assuming that Estelles's experience is centred around 'spiritualism' and a belief that, as a medium, she can provide a link between this world and the spirit world. Spirits can use her as a vessel, communicating in writing through her hand but not her conscious mind. She went on to explain that, during a five-day period in early 1970, she had awoken each day to a growing list of names and dates, crudely scrawled across the wallpaper on the wall adjacent to her bed. Her parents were understandably unhappy that their daughter had taken to defacing her bedroom and while she protested her innocence at first, an encounter with the spirit of a gentleman who would introduce himself as William Avery, made her view the situation in a different light.

Estelle didn't make it entirely clear exactly how the encounter with Avery manifested (whether it was in something akin to a lucid dream or more of a traditional encounter), however, he explained that, through her, he had been responsible for the writings and that the names on the walls were those of his family and other local families that had lived when he had resided in the house. Estelle also recalled how unapologetic he was, saying that "it was his house, and he was at liberty to do what he liked in it". Avery was born in the house in 1677 and had been a wool trader in the town, becoming deeply attached to the property and finally passing in ungiven circumstances in the mid-1700s. Estelle told me that for a period, Avery was a very restless spirit who would complain that due to the pain and poor circulation in his 'blessed legs' he dare not rest and had to keep on walking. A charming turn of phrase that resonated with me as my own legs very much ached having been on them all that morning.

Although, her story did not have the time to reach a proper conclusion in the near hour that we chatted, she spoke of other mysterious happenings and "bumps in the night" that occurred during this period which I'm afraid I failed to capture in sufficient detail to merit retelling. I haven't been able to verify Estelle's story, nor have I been able to contact her since. I had been keen to follow up so I could take a full and proper account of all the happenings she discussed. I haven't been able to find a medium operating by that name in the local area either. She may operate under a pseudonym or may just choose not to monetise her gift.

The encounter was unexpected to say the least and although I can't explain how Estelle knew of my endeavours, 'cold calling' techniques used by mediums have been well documented and extensively explained by many people including the popular mentalist Derren Brown in his excellent book 'Tricks of the Mind'. I was also drawn to thinking of the infamous case of Borley Rectory in the 1930s, at one time known as the "Most Haunted House in England". Happenings are alleged to have been rife even prior to **Reverend Lionel Algernon Foyster and his wife Marianne moving into the house** along with their adopted daughter Adelaide (Foyster was first cousin of the Bull family whom the manor had belonged to since the mid-1800s). The activities experienced by Foyster and his wife were made more famous however, as they were documented by paranormal researcher; Harry Price, sent to the property on behalf of the Daily Mirror. Price would document a myriad of activity, the case making him famous in his own right, including how Marianne Foyster would receive strange messages on the walls of the rectory through the process of automatic writings – alleged spirit pleas and requests for her to "please get help" for them. As it turned out, Marianne Foyster and other inhabitants of the manor would eventually admit their role in a big hoax, for her part she confessed that she faked the phenomena to divert attention away from her affair with the lodger.

I offer these potential explanations, not to discredit Estelle and other mediums but to provide a balance and potential alternate explanation to the gifts that some people claim to be blessed with. I retain a healthy cynicism, but Estelle stood to gain nothing financially from our meeting and I'm certain that there was no element of intended trickery about the encounter either. For my part I did learn one very valuable lesson and now always carry a notepad and pencil with me wherever I go. You never know when you're going to hear your next ghost tale, so always be prepared to record it.

CHAPTER 1

EMSCOTE

In the mid-17th Century Emscote contained only a Manor House. This was a stone building originally thought to be medieval. Any remnants of the building with its pointed arch, oak staircase, panelled rooms, and gothic windows are now long gone. By 1870 Emscote (or Edmonscott) was still just a hamlet in the parish of Milverton. At the time, British writer John Marius Wilson's Imperial Gazetter of England highlighted what would have been a modern Wesleyan Chapel "built here in 1863; in the Lombardic style of red brick, varied with blue and yellow brick, and Bath stone dressings" as a particular feature of note within the hamlet.

Modern day Emscote is a very different place. Part of Warwick District and sitting midway between Warwick and Leamington, it roughly extends from the Portobello Bridge (or Emscote Bridge) to Coten End. The Emscote Road is a very busy residential and increasingly commercial thoroughfare which during commuter periods can become very congested. The Portobello Bridge was built in the late 1820s across the river Avon to create a direct toll-free route from Leamington to Warwick.

The first tale of supernatural activity in the Emscote area is known to occur at a different bridge — Emscote Road Bridge, number 46, which spans the Grand Union Canal. Locals will know Emscote Road Bridge as the 'Tesco Bridge' due its immediate proximity to the large supermarket. Older residents will perhaps remember the bridge for different reasons. Emscote Mill once stood adjacent to the canal bridge. Not to be confused with the Emscote gelatine Mill in Wharf Street or Rock Mills on the Leamington side of the Portobello Bridge, Emscote Mill was built on the north bank of the canal in 1806 and was operated by the company of Kench & Sons until 1961. An overshot waterwheel was driven by excess water from the adjacent canal. This was replaced by a steam engine in the 1850s. In 1905 the Mill was reconstructed and completely modernised. From 1918 the mill was driven by electric motors. In 1961 the mill was shut down and the machinery removed. Shortly after the building was converted into the fondly remembered Fleur de Lys pie factory.

Originally baked at the Fleur de Lys pub at Lowsonford a few miles outside of Warwick by a Mr Brookes (or his chef) in the 1950s, the delicious steak & kidney or chicken & mushroom pies were legendary in the area. After Mr Brookes moved production to the old Emscote Mill in Warwick, next to the canal Bridge and expanded the business nation-wide. The pie factory was demolished in the early 1990s and, was replaced by residential apartments that collectively form the appropriately named "Fleur De Lys Court."

It was on a late summers evening in the early 1900s when two local cyclists paused for breath on the Emscote Road canal bridge. While taking refreshment and enjoying the beautiful sunset, one of the cyclists noticed something floating in the still canal water below. They leaned over the bridge wall together to identify the mystery object, which they eventually determined to be a child's hat. Scrambling down the path to the waterside, the pair hoped to retrieve the article so that they could leave it where it might be found by its owner, saving them from disappointment or perhaps the wrath of an angry parent. Once on the towpath however, the hat was nowhere to be seen and no amount of fishing around with a tree branch could locate it.

Several weeks later a lady crossing the same bridge had a similar experience while walking her dog in heavy rain. On this occasion the elderly woman thought she could see a child on the towpath, attempting to retrieve an object floating on the surface of the murky water. She called out to the child to be careful but received not so much as a glance from the small figure. Her concern was such that she summoned a youth loitering on the far side of the bridge and politely asked him to assist. The young man duly obliged but returned from the towpath telling the lady that there was no one there. Thinking she must have been mistaken due to the inclement weather she continued her way.

On another occasion a family were crossing the bridge when the father of the group became concerned at seeing a very young child, sitting on the edge of the canal bank dangling his little feet in the water. The man called out anxiously, warning the child to take care before the toddler suddenly disappeared from his sight. As he raced to the water's edge, he was followed by several family members. There was no sign of a child or any disturbance in the canal at all. The father was calmed by those present with him, none of whom had borne any witness to the vision that the father believed he had seen. Events that occurred in July 1891 may provide an explanation for all the above happenings.

It was a sunny Saturday afternoon, and local boat builder Edwin Roberts was working on a boat on the canal at Emscote not far from bridge number 46. He was suddenly distracted by the sound of children and looking up saw two young boys. It was just before one o'clock and the boys were playing on the towing-path of the canal about a hundred yards on the Leamington side of the bridge. It was a Saturday and it appeared that the youngsters had wandered down from their homes in Emscote to seek adventure by the water. The children, later identified as three-year-old Alfred Fennell and Richard Ward who was six, were playing very close to the edge of the canal. Concerned for their safety, Mr Roberts told them to leave the water's edge. After losing sight of them, and assuming they had done as he had told them to, he was happy that they were out of harm's way.

About an hour later, Mr Robert's employer; a Mr Farr, appeared in a state of high anxiety, informing him that another boatman believed a young boy may have fallen into the canal. The two men went to investigate and found six-year-old Richard, whom Mr Roberts immediately recognised, standing alone under the bridge. As they questioned him over the whereabouts of his little friend, he said he was "in there" — pointing at the time to the water — adding in a painfully childish manner that "he was waiting for him to come out again so they could go home". Ominously, a child's hat was floating in the area to which Richard was pointing. It didn't take long for the boatmen to find the younger child beneath the surface of the water and once retrieved they laid him on the towing-path and tried to restore life. Sadly, it was evident that the life of the small child had fled. The young boy, Alfred Fennell was the son of Mr George Fennell, a carter from nearby Humphries Street.

As was the case in those days inquests into such tragedies were generally held at the nearest public house to where the incident had occurred. The Inn or pub was central to the effective administration of local justice in the eighteenth and nineteenth centuries, until the rise of the police courts. In many communities the Inn or pub was the only readily available large indoor space where public events could take place. Auctions were commonly held in pubs so were the petty sessions (the forerunner of magistrate's courts) and coroners' inquests. The proceedings were normally held upstairs or in the back room of the pub, sometimes with their own entrances so that the magistrate or coroner had no need to pass through the beer swilling public. The sounds of conviviality and the aroma of tobacco and alcohol would have inevitably pervaded the proceedings though. Pub justice was lucrative for landlords who benefited from payment for the room and the increased custom petty sessions and inquests invariably brought, with locals and witnesses quenching both their curiosity and thirst. Charles Dickens commented in his novel Bleak House that "The coroner frequents more public houses than any man alive".

So, it was in this case that the inquest was held at the Emscote Tavern, where the body of the boy had been taken on the Monday afternoon after the accident. The father of the deceased said that the boy was three years old last September and, as young as he was, had just started attending All Saints school. Mr Fennell had quickly been advised of the tragedy and had rushed to the Emscote Tavern where the body had been taken. Richard Ward was understandably considered too young to give an accurate account of the tragedy, and the inquest returned a verdict of "accidentally drowned". The coroner remarked that it was a pity that the little children had both been allowed to wander. A juryman also endorsed this sentiment, adding "it wanted a little care on the part of the mothers".

The unexplained fleeting glimpses of both the child and the floating hat seen from the bridge by passersby, all seem linked to this terrible incident.

⁂

If you walk up Castle Hill towards the Eastgate in Warwick, you may notice two plaques on the walls of the Warwick almshouses. The more ancient of the two commemorates Thomas Oken and Nicholas Eyffler, benefactors of the town. The second and more recent addition is to the memory of a well-known "Gentleman of Warwick" who sadly died in 2011 at the age of 84. Mr Roger Smith bequeathed his beloved home "Melrose" in Emscote Road to the benefit of the charities of Thomas Oken and Nicholas Eyffler and the almshouses were modernised in 2014 because of Roger's generosity.

Roger lived at his Emscote Home for 82 years and was very well-known in the town. He had a great love for and long-established interest in Warwick. An Old Warwickian (the name given to former pupils of Warwick School) he

6

enlisted in the Royal Navy aged 17 and subsequently joined a newly built ship, HMS Porlock to which he became very attached. He later wrote a book entitled 'Shipshape and Bristol Fashion' which recalled his happy naval days. A man of many interests, he was prominent in many local organisations and associations. Roger became a senior local government officer with Stratford District Council, during which time I personally got to know him well.

It was in his house in Emscote Road (which Roger often referred to as "Dear old Melrose"), that he was happiest. Following his passing, the new owners of the property soon fell similarly in love with it. The house always felt warm and welcoming and for many months, nothing out of the ordinary occurred. Frequent unexplained activity suddenly became a regular occurrence though. The residents of the property experienced unaccountable sounds of footsteps and knocking. They also experienced the sensations of being visited and occasionally touched by an unseen presence. On one occasion a member of the household felt their bottom being patted while they were alone in the kitchen! The owners record how, despite these strange happenings, they never felt frightened or intimidated. Familiar with the property's history, they even took to telling 'Roger' off for his playful disturbances, convinced that the bond the late owner had with the house was so strong that his spirit had never left it.

More recently the figure of a woman in a long grey dress has been seen on several occasions, climbing the stairs. Her identity is a complete mystery though. Although peculiarity pervades the house, the current owners feel privileged to be custodians of it and are more than happy to share their space with the spirit of the dear old gentleman who called ' Melrose' home for so many years,

❧

Warwick has over the years lost many of its pubs and drinking establishments. Research reveals references to between 120 and 130 pubs of which only around a quarter remain. Older residents of the town will recall some but the names of many have been lost forever. Over time Smith Street alone has seen eight different pubs. But the curious events at one pub between 1934 and the early 1940s are captured in folklore.

Ansell's Brewery took over The Dolphin Inn in Warwick when they acquired the old Leamington Spa brewery of Lucas & Co. Ltd in 1928. The Dolphin Inn was situated at number 32 Emscote Road on the eastern corner of Pickard Street and was one of more than 120 tied houses to be acquired in the business deal. Tied houses were required to buy at least some their products from a particular brewery or pub company as opposed to a free house that could purchase its products from wherever it wanted. At one time Pickard Street with its neighbour Avon Street had a reputation for being perhaps not the most salubrious area of the town. It is alleged that even the police would only patrol the area in pairs.

The establishment was run for many years by Alfred (Bert) and Maud Inglefield. As well as running the pub Bert worked as a wheelwright. This craftsman's trade of building and repairing wooden wheels had been conducted at the rear of the premises by previous landlords. The pub was instantly recognisable owing to its unusual colourful sign depicting a Dolphin leaping out of the water. Certainly not a sight one would normally associate with such a land locked town. On the corner of the building there was a cellar trap, and the building also housed a workshop in which Bert conducted his trade as a wheelwright. Next door at number 34 was a butcher's shop owned by Percy and Marjorie Clamp. As was the case in those days Percy had inherited the business from his father.

There is story that for a few years from around 1935 locals at the Dolphin reported seeing fleeting glimpses of a scruffy man who would approach the steps of the pub before suddenly disappearing into thin air. The man wore a long thick coat with what appeared to be a bloodstained scarf tightly bound around his neck. Some suggest it was the ghost of William Kitchener.

William Kitchener was a former licensee of The Volunteer Inn in Smith Street Warwick. He was well known in the town and a prominent member of the Ancient Order of Foresters. He had joined the Court Dudley in 1890 and was secretary to the organisation. He had occupied many positions of authority in the town and at one time was Chief Ranger of the district. Kitchener lived at 28 Emscote Road, Warwick, two doors away from the Dolphin Inn.

In July 1934 William was found dead in the garden adjoining his house with wounds to his throat. The gruesome discovery was made by Bert Inglefield at around 9.30am in the morning and a bloodstained razor was found beneath the body of the deceased man. The shock of the terrible event left Mrs Kitchener in such a dreadful state that she was completely unable to assist the local police with their investigations into the tragedy and could never bring herself to speak about it. William Kitchener had been unemployed since being stood down as licensee of the Volunteer Inn and it's not clear if his wounds were self-inflicted or caused by the hands of others. What is known is that he was a regular drinker at the Dolphin Inn so the circumstantial evidence certainly suggests that he may well have been the mystery figure seen by locals, still trying to take the short walk from number 28 to number 32 Emscote Road after his horrific demise.

❧

Running parallel to Pickard Street is Avon Street. Records show that houses in Avon Street (originally named Margett's Street) were being erected in 1834 and together with Pickard Place, Pickard Street and Goodhall Street formed an island of terrace development between St. Nicholas Meadow (now known as St. Nicholas Park) and the canal. During my childhood and by many previous generations, the park was always referred to in local tongue as 'the meda'.

It is more commonly referred to these days as 'St Nick's Park'. Following a change in employment my father moved the family to number 61 Avon Street in the early 1960s. At that time, it was a stereotypical English terraced street with close knit families living cheek by jowl and always looking out for each other. There were two chapels in the vicinity and Mrs Webb's and Tommy Morris's corner shops catered for all your needs. 'The meda' was the ultimate children's playground where kids would play from dusk 'til dawn without the fears that seem to prevail in the modern-day world. Gossip was rife and nothing went unnoticed by the streets local 'neighbourhood watch' ladies dressed in their everyday pinafores and headscarves as they chitter-chattered away, arms always folded.

You could guarantee that if you had been up to mischief your mum would know about it long before you got home with a resulting 'thick ear' the likely outcome. At the bottom of the street were some run down terraced two up, two down houses barricaded in by high rusty corrugated metal sheets. Behind an old Victorian wall were the remnants of what would have been fine orchards and allotments which led down to the river. In times of flooding, it was not uncommon to see rats in the street. At the rear of the terrace, we lived in was open farmland which had been a piggery owned by a local farmer known as 'bandy' Cleaver. He had acquired his local soubriquet since his legs were so bowed, he would never be able to 'stop a pig in a passage'.

The site was eventually sold by Mr. Cleaver and the housing development known as Emscote Gardens was built on it. There were always stories of ghosts and hauntings in the street and kids used to say the dark passages running between the houses had all kinds of evil ghosts and goblins lurking in them. The truth was of course that it was the kids themselves that provided the spooky noises whilst running up and down the 'jitties', much to the annoyance of the adjoining residents. One old gentleman by the name of Mr Bonehill would always shout and attempt to chase the children much to their delight. Running the gauntlet of 'Bonehill's passage' without getting caught was always a challenge for the more audacious kids. Mr Bonehill's walking stick packed a hefty whack to those unlucky enough to get cornered by him. A large family called the Henson's lived opposite and the children claimed their house was haunted. They would put on displays for the kids in the street by hiding beneath the windows and throwing dish cloths and rags in the air claiming they were ghosts. Somewhat ironically their house was struck by lightning one stormy winters night, but fortunately no one was hurt. Little did we know at that time, there really was a haunted house in the street.

In the early 1980s my brother Paul and his wife Sue bought their first house and returned to Avon Street, the street of our shared childhood. Only a few doors away from where we had spent many happy years growing up, the house was a perfect start for them. Absolutely pristine, the property had been the pride and joy for a long time of a Mr and Mrs Pewsey. Sadly, Mr Pewsey had passed away and his wife Amy, at the time in her late 80s, had decided to sell their cherished home. A good-sized family home, the house had two downstairs rooms, three decent sized bedrooms and the bonus of a useful dry cellar. Initially they didn't think they had been successful in securing the property as their offer had been less than at least two other bids. It came as a wonderful surprise when the agents contacted them to say that, despite their lower offer, Mrs. Pewsey wanted them to have the property.

From the very beginning Paul maintains that somehow, they always felt the house had found them and unlike current day property buying, things moved quickly. In a very short period, they received the keys. Even the moving in process was seamless as Mrs. Pewsey had already moved out to live with her daughter. On opening the front door for the first time Paul and Sue were greeted by a pile of 'welcome to your new home' cards and, after their first cup of tea, they set about opening them. To their delight there was one from Mrs. Pewsey wishing them years of joy and happiness in their new home. The greeting did however end with a slightly strange statement:

'You know the spirits chose you don't you … so you will always be watched over and safe in that house'.

Amy Pewsey was known to be a devout Christian lady, so possibly such sentiments were just part of her kind demeanor.

As the first Christmas in the house approached cards from family and friends began to arrive. One morning an envelope postmarked Newbury dropped through the letter box. It was a Christmas card from Mrs Pewsey, extending season's greetings, and her pleasure in knowing that they had settled in well. Letters continued to arrive periodically with the elderly lady's correspondence always implying that she somehow knew how life was in the house. Paul and Sue just put this down to her advanced years and perhaps just a little eccentricity.

During the first few months in the house all was indeed well although both agreed that occasionally they felt that they were not alone in the house. Nothing sinister or unnerving, just this inexplicable sense of something or somebody else being present. These intermittent occurrences often coincided with their pet cat Oscar behaving in an out of character way. Normally an extremely passive creature, he would suddenly leap up and become transfixed on something unseen in the room. Unusual as this had never previously been a feature of his erstwhile laid-back demeanour.

Becoming nonchalant to the feeling of a third party in the house, life, aside from Oscar's occasionally odd behaviour, continued as normal until one night when they were both awoken by a loud thud and the sound of heavy footsteps right outside the bedroom door. My brother was convinced there was an intruder in the house and summoned up all his courage to fling open the bedroom door, fully anticipating confrontation with a burglar. To his astonishment there was no sign of anyone or anything there. Confused but hugely relieved, both Paul and Sue searched the house. They found no sign of forced entry, and nothing was disturbed. Even Oscar slept soundly in his basket. They are adamant to this day that there was someone else in the house that night though and the memory of the frightening experience still haunts them.

The occasional minor incident continued to occur, albeit often with a potentially rational explanation. Household items would go missing for short periods of time and lights would suddenly dim or switch off. One further major incident, however, remains completely unexplainable all these years later. One evening whilst watching TV a distinct smell of burning started to waft through the house. The very unpleasant chemical odour was accompanied by toxic fumes which Paul immediately recognised as electrical. The source appeared to be coming from the cellar. It was soon discovered that the somewhat dated fuse box was smouldering dramatically and panic set in.

The well used British axiom, 'Sod's Law', infers that 'if something can go wrong, it will' and sometimes has the accompanying corollary, that 'misfortune will always happen at the worst possible time'. This was certainly the case that evening. When an attempt was made to call the emergency services it was discovered that the home phone line was dead. With no mobile phone and fumes beginning to fill the house, my brother ran the several hundred metres to the public phone box at the top of the street on the Emscote Road. Despite these frantic efforts to contact the fire brigade, the line from the phone box to his horror, also appeared to be down. As he ran home, desperately wondering what to do next, Paul was astonished to see two fire engines and fire crews present and already attending the incident. Sue greeted him warmly congratulating him on his swift action and the amazing promptness of the emergency services.

Totally bewildered, he explained that he hadn't been able to raise the alarm and, as no one else had been aware of the incident, could not reason how the emergency services had been summoned. The fire crew confirmed that they had been asked to attend but subsequent enquiries failed to identify the source of the alert. How prophetic then were the words of Mrs Pewsey in her card welcoming the couple to the home that she wanted them to have:

'You know the spirits chose you don't you ... so you will always be watched over and safe in that house. '

"

Millions of spiritual creatures walk the earth unseen,
both when we wake, and when we sleep ...'

John Milton (1608–1674)

CHAPTER 2

NORTHGATE STREET REVISITED

Northgate Street has always played a prominent role in the activities of central Warwick. The street is so named due to its proximity to the original northern entrance to the town via the North Gate which was demolished at the end of the thirteenth century.

In the summer of 1572 Queen Elizabeth I, processed along the street on her way to meet Robert Dudley Earl of Leicester, it being enroute from Warwick to Kenilworth Castle. On 5th September 1694 the houses in the street were destroyed by the Great Fire of Warwick but they were reconstructed very soon after. The street was renamed Sheep Street in the late 17th Century when the cattle and sheep market was temporarily relocated there. The street reverted to being called Northgate Street in 1823 when the cattle market was moved to Coten End. During the late 19th and early 20th century, some of the properties on the street were acquired by Warwickshire County and many local people will remember them as The Education Department which was established there in the 1930s.

The beautiful houses you see today were built as the result of an Act of Parliament which stipulated that houses destroyed by the fire should be rebuilt two stories high of brick or stone and with oak door cases and window frames. Many of the original internal features of the houses have been unaltered since the seventeenth century and the external structures too have remained as they were first built. The entire eastern side of the street has recently been totally and sympathetically restored providing up market homes for 21st century living whilst maintaining the look of the original 'William and Mary' to mid-Georgian houses.

A chilling tale dating back to the mid-1800s was once told by a local schoolmaster living in one of the grand properties at the time. The master, who taught classics at nearby Warwick school (the oldest boy's school in England) had been working late in his study. Several hours after sunset, he had gathered up his books for the night and, carrying a lamp, began making his way through the dark hallway to the front of the house. As his lamp illuminated the passage, he saw at the far end a man's face. He instantly assumed that a thief had got into the house.

The possibility of this had occurred to him before as a gentleman of relative wealth in an uneven society. That burglary was still rife despite it being an offence potentially punishable by death, was testament to the desperation of some. He had always felt the rear of the property was unsecure and to protect both himself and his property, the master had always kept an English Flintlock pocket pistol in his desk. Quickly retrieving the weapon, and holding the lamp cautiously in his free hand, he returned to the hallway. Finding it now empty, he assumed the intruder had made his way into the drawing room however, the drawing room too appeared unoccupied. The large room was cluttered with bookcases and furniture, so the master continued to proceed warily. He called out loudly several times to the intruder to show himself, as much in hope of attracting the attention of a passing policeman as in expectation of drawing the prowler.

Suddenly a face peered around one of the bookcases. Extremely pallid and hairless, the orbits of the eyes were sunken. The overall appearance of the figure was odd, the body attached to the face appearing to be immersed in the bookcase itself. As the master advanced closer, the strange figure became more recognisable as an old man, his shoulders very hunched. Appearing to emerge slowly from the side of the bookcase, the old man shuffled away from the gaze of the master in absolute silence, back turned and narrow gait gaining pace as he headed towards a small adjoining closet. With trembling pistol and lamp in hand, the master followed the old man but found the little closet empty as he pulled a door open uneasily. There was a tiny window at the rear of the closet, but it was closed and fastened. In any event not even a cat could have got through it. That there was no intruder in the closet was impossibly astonishing. Perplexed by the strange episode the master undertook a rigorous investigation of the whole house seeking rational explanation to the occurrence. He found none.

Living in such close proximity to St Mary's church and being well acquainted with the local clergy, the master sought out the church verger the following day in an attempt to lighten the burden of his troubling experience. The response he did not anticipate. After giving a description of what he had seen to the verger, the attendant replied in a very matter of fact manner.

"That will be Old George. You are certainly not the first to have seen him".

The verger compounded the master's disbelief further by describing the gentleman's hunched, shuffling gait. The phantom of 'George' had been seen on numerous occasions in and around Northgate Street. A consensus among those who had seen him had been reached that, his most peculiar features, notably his lack of hair and eyebrows, must have been the consequence of some form of fire or gunpowder explosion – an accident or incident which presumably claimed his mortal life. Several attempts had been made to help him find peace and move on but all without success. 'Old George' may perhaps still wander Northgate Street today, in search of justice for his untimely demise.

CHAPTER 3

CHURCH STREET

"

'Fire broake out about two of the clock in the afternoon on the Fifth of this instant September,in the western part of the town of Warwick, which by the violence of the wind was soe swiftly carried through the principall parts of the same that noe opposition could be made to hinder the fierceness of its progress, till it had in a few hours consumed almost all of the High Street, the Church Street and the Sheep street intirely, part of the Jury Street Newstreet, and many buildings about the Market House, together with the great and antient church of St. Maryes and severall other buildings on other parts of the towne ...'

**Account from The Commissioners' Order Book,
the Great Fire of Warwick**

It is said that the great fire of Warwick in 1694 led to an urban design revolution of the town and caused builders to review the way in which buildings were constructed. The fire had destroyed many houses along the High Street, Market Street, Castle Street and swept up Church Street to eventually severely damage St Mary's Church. The tower, knave and transept of the church were destroyed but the chancel, chapter house and the Beauchamp Chapel were saved. Interestingly a draft of the proposals for the new buildings and church were sent to the office of legendary English Architect Sir Christopher Wren for consideration in February 1695. Wren, remembered most for the design of St Paul's Cathedral & The Monument in London, subsequently received £10 for his observations on the church design.

The post fire properties no longer displayed jetted facades and the concept of timber framed construction in which floors of buildings overhung each other was not replicated. The stunning buildings we see today are credited to Francis and William Smith. William was given the position of surveyor for the fire council and took a lead role in overseeing the rebuilding project. Francis joined his brother in the reconstruction of the church and later became a successful architect, overseeing the building of the new Courthouse in Warwick too. The brothers had a lasting impact on the rebuilding post fire Warwick evidenced by the beautiful architecture we see today. Much of the rebuilding of the houses in Church Street was undertaken in 1704, the same year in which the reconstruction of the tower of St Mary's was completed.

Many residents of these early 18th century buildings have experienced unexplained paranormal activity over the years, but it is the owner of one particular property who has experienced perhaps the strangest occurrences in the street. The well-known antique dealership was established in the 1860s and moved to its current premises in 1974. The property boasts beautiful Georgian showrooms and has its own restoration workshop. The dealership specialises in Georgian (18th and early 19th century) English furniture but fine art, mirrors, barometers, and many more period pieces can be found too. The current owner and her late husband were so taken by the property that they bought it at auction without fully exploring the site prior to purchase. It wasn't until after completion of the deal that the previous owner advised the new owners against spending time in the allegedly haunted, upper part of the house.

On entering the building one gets the instant impression of stepping back in time. A cavernous hallway greets you and your eye is immediately drawn to the magnificent winding wooden staircase and balustrade that entices you to climb it to explore the upper floors. The aroma of wax and polish fills the air, and the downstairs rooms are an eclectic ensemble of antique furniture. The gardens and outbuilding are an unexpected delight. Running almost the length of the ornamental period garden is a building thought to be from the Cromwellian period. Intriguingly alongside the building is what appears to be a section of cobbled road, possibly part of the original high street running from Church Street to Swan Street. It is a feature that feels peculiarly out of kilter with the main building that was built later in 1704. The cellars of the building are dank and eerie and used for the storage of random items such as odd chairs or parts of old clocks. The remains of an old well have been uncovered in the cellar too. A relic that conceivably provides a gateway for the dead to communicate with the living.

We are all familiar with seeing water used to create energy and power. Historically this was used to drive water wheels, and, in the modern day, we harness the energy of water in creating hydroelectric power. Most of us will also be able to testify to the regenerative effect that drinking a large glass of cold water can have on a hot summer day. In paranormal circles, there are many theories centered around water. Some say spirits can draw upon the energy found within water, enabling them to physically interact with the living world. Debates are rife about quite how exactly this might be done but proponents of such theories, highlight how reports of anomalous activity, poltergeists and hauntings are often increased in areas where humidity is higher than average. There are many other mysteries associated with bodies of water throughout the world too, such as the well know Bermuda Triangle in the Western part of the North Atlantic Ocean, where water and the unknown are synonymous.

The first indication of any unusual activity at the house transpired when an antique barometer, hung on the wall at the top of the first flight of stairs, was found removed from its bracket and propped against the wall. The glass cover had been completely removed. There was no indication that it had fallen as, other than the missing glass, the item was perfectly intact. The pins securing the glass front were still in place and not bent or twisted in any way. There was no sign however of the missing glass cover.

One morning, soon after this strangeness, the owners returned from walking their dog to find that, as they attempted to unlock the door, the chain had also been secured in place, preventing them from regaining access to their home. Fastening the inside chain after leaving the property for their morning walk would have been impossible and, although they had a friend staying with their son at the time, neither had any cause to secure the building whilst the owners were out. Their friend was surprised to be summoned to unchain the door by the calling of the owners. He hadn't chained the door, and although there is always the possibility that his young son had been responsible, he didn't believe this to be the case, leaving everybody mystified by the event.

In the bathroom, there was a brief period where copious amounts of torn paper would regularly be found littering the floor without explanation. The family decided to seek the advice of a local medium after an acquaintance suggested that a poltergeist may be responsible for the strange activity.

A thorough investigation of the property was subsequently undertaken, and, to the astonishment of the owners, the medium claimed that they were being haunted by the spirit of a restless governess named Elizabeth and a disobedient young girl whom the tutoress spent her days chasing and chastising. The family subsequently had the property 'cleansed' by a member of the clergy and strange happenings now rarely occur. The owners do, however, still occasionally glimpse unexplained shadows in the upper rooms.

A short while after I had been offered the above tale, an unrelated local gentleman who refers to himself as a spirit medium, coincidentally told me of an experience of his own relating to the very same property on Church Street. Late one summers evening and after visiting friends at a nearby house, he passed the property and paused suddenly as his attention became drawn to what he described as a pale girl. Around twelve years of age, she beckoned him from one of the ground floor windows. As he drew closer, he says that the image of the girl, dressed in Victorian attire, faded, and was then suddenly gone.

"

'At first cock-crow the ghosts must go back to their
quiet graves below'

Theodosia Garrison (1874 – 1944)

❧

Throughout history an-
tiques, and mirrors specifically, have been surrounded
by superstition and haunted
tales. Born in Warwick into
a family with a long history in the antique business
John, now retired, has recently passed the company
onto his two sons who will
be the fourth generation to
run the business. Although
no longer in Warwick, the
successful family of dealers still have premises in London and
Edinburgh. Over the years John had amassed considerable
expertise, particularly in antique furniture, clocks, and ceramics.
However, there is one specialism that he has fought shy of
after a very strange experience he had over thirty years ago.
In the early years of his trading John developed a penchant
for antique mirrors and successfully bought and sold some
very fine examples, both British and continental.

When a friend and fellow antique dealer contacted him to say he had just returned from France, and amongst several pieces he had purchased from auction was a particularly ornate 18th Century mirror, despite its rather hefty price tag John just had to have it. The auction listing had described the mirror as a 'stunning example of its era with lightly foxed glass demonstrating the pleasing patina of age'. It had 'wood glazing beads from the early Regency period, adorning the frame in a berain decoration, as well as four shells in the spandrels. A rich ornamentation of acanthus leaves, volutes and gadoons enhancing the large, surmounted pediment, the whole piece topped with a beautiful openwork shell'. So taken was he with this description and his subsequent purchase, John decided not to sell the mirror on as it would be a perfect addition to his grandiose Victorian Warwick home. John's wife Barbara was also absolutely delighted with the luxurious mirror which was carefully mounted above the fireplace in the sitting room.

The ancient Romans believed that any reflective surface, including mirrors, reflected the human soul and must never be misused as the consequences would result in terrible misfortune and the soul could be lost for eternity. Some cultures even believe that mirrors are portals to other worlds, predictors of the future and windows to the afterlife. Certain civilizations still believe that mirrors watch us as we gaze into them, acting as a two-way viewing screen to other dimensions. A belief in Chinese culture is that if you carry a corpse past a mirror, it will become a ghost. Dutch and German cultures have a more eerie superstition. If you see your reflection anywhere immediately after a loved one has passed, it is an omen that you will be the next to pass. For hundreds of years the traditional practice of covering mirrors in a house where a loved one is not long for this world or has just passed, has been observed by many cultures. There has always been a superstition that one might see death or the devil himself in the reflection coming to gather the soul of the soon to be departed. On a more practical and earthly level, the covering of mirrors ensures that gatherers and mourners focus on the departing or departed and are not unnecessarily distracted by their own image or appearance.

A few days after the new mirror had been proudly mounted in the sitting room, Barbara was hurriedly leaving the house as she was running late for a hairdresser's appointment in the town. Pausing briefly to glance in the mirror to check her appearance, she was left astonished. There was no image reflecting at her in the glass. Transfixed and momentarily rooted to the spot, a few seconds passed before her face emerged to stare back at her. Affected by the incident, her husband understandably dismissed her tale as nonsense.

Some weeks later, much to his surprise John was also to experience the same phenomena as his wife. One evening on entering the sitting room he casually glanced at the mirror in passing to switch on the TV. After a double take, he too became aware that his image had not been reflected in the glass. Again, as with his wife's previous experience, following several seconds of confusion, his face slowly emerged to stare back at him. In attempting to try to find a rational explanation, John lifted the mirror from its mounting and carefully examined the front and back. Apart from some minor signs of wear consistent with its age, the mirror was soundly constructed with no hint of anything that might produce any kind of optical illusion. After sharing his experience with his wife, the couple both began to feel uneasy about the mirror and almost became afraid to look into it.

Although uncommon, there are several recognised phobias associated with mirrors. Eisotrophia, spectrophobia, and catoptrophobia are sometimes used interchangeably and, although all are all terms used to describe morbid fears of mirrors, there is a distinction between each condition. Eisotrophobia sufferers have a fear of their own reflection, spectrophobia is specific to a fear of the reflection in mirrors and those with catoptrophobia are phobic of anything reflective. With both spectrophobia and catotophobia, sufferers have abnormal and persistent anxieties which result in a variety of fears. These include fears of seeing ghosts in the mirror, anxiety around breaking mirrors (because of the associated bad luck) and irrational worries that something, or someone is lurking within the mirror, waiting for their opportunity to leap out and drag individuals into the other side. All disorders can be quite serious, leading individuals to peculiar and extreme avoidance behaviours, resulting in disruption to all aspects of their life.

The strange events escalated to a whole new level when Barbara was applying the finishing touches to her makeup one evening. As she manoeuvred her lipstick, she suddenly realised that her image was static and wasn't reflecting any movement. It was just staring motionless back at her. She yelled for her husband to attend immediately, but by the time he arrived her image was once again reflecting normally. This time John didn't doubt his wife's word as the incident had left her hysterical and traumatised.

Questioning the reality of their shared experiences, John & Barbara discussed whether they should get rid of the mirror or perhaps try to live with it a bit longer to see if any further strange activity occurred. The dramatic climax to this story occurred shortly before Christmas. The couple were busily decorating their grand house ready for the family Yuletide get together. To complete the festive ensemble their attention was drawn to the mirror. They jokingly agreed that in order not to 'upset' it they would merely lightly decorate the antique with a length of gold tinsel topped with a sprig of holly. The tinsel wound around the ornate frame, and as they stretched to place the holly, there in the mirrored glass behind their own reflections, appeared the face and upper torso of an austere looking woman dressed in period attire. This incident proved the coup de grace for the mirror, which was quickly removed from the wall and sold by John at auction shortly afterwards.

It is difficult to find a rational or scientific explanation for these accounts. Early mirrors were made with a silver backing which made them turn black over a period as the silver oxidised. This process resulted in a mirror taking on an otherworldly appearance leading the naked eye to sometimes see ghostly shapes or figures forming in the distorted glass. As condensation forms on glass, fog and blotches can appear, which over generations, has further propelled myths of phantoms and paranormal beings manifesting themselves.

Lighting also impacts on how we observe images. Candlelight or low light can cause the human eye to create forms or shapes that are not actually there, and lighting position can distort or refract images in peculiar, unexpected, and unsettling ways.

The phenomenon of 'sensory habituation' may also offer some grasping form of explanation. This can occur when an individual is presented with a constant sound, image, or odour. This may be most relatable with smells; for example, the scent of flowers, or food and drink in a room, is often very noticeable on entering but the same scents fade after being in the room for a while. The scents will however, become very apparent again on leaving and re-entering the very same room. It is difficult to imagine a scenario where you might become so familiar with your own reflection that it would disappear though.

So, if you are tempted to buy that beautiful mirror you saw in the antique shop in Warwick, perchance you would be wise to think carefully about your purchase and what you may or may not see staring back at you from it.

"

'For now we see in a mirror dimly, but then
face to face'

-1 Corinthians 13:1

CHAPTER 4

SALTISFORD REVISITED

A s you pass along Bir-
mingham Road and
under the railway bridge
towards Warwick town
centre, you can easily miss
what might appear to be
the remains of an old barn,
set back some way from the
highway in scrubland. Scaf-
folded and partially covered,
the unremarkable external
appearance belies the historical significance of this site. More
noticeable is the ancient 'Chapel of St Michael' that abuts the
pavement. The buildings are the last remnants in the country
of what was once a leper house.

Leprosy (now known as Hansen's Disease) is a devastat-
ing condition that can inflict extreme physical deformity and
discomfort on its victims. It is an infection caused by slow

growing bacteria called mycobacterium leprae, effecting the nerves, skin, eyes, and lining of the nose. The root causes of the disease are today understood and can be treated. In the Middle Ages however, its appearance often provoked considerable misunderstanding. Definitions of leprosy changed dramatically between AD 1000 and 1500 and the disease was often a 'catch all' for a wide range of conditions. Medieval perceptions of lepra probably differ significantly from those of modern Hansen's disease but, even so, the actual word 'leper' is still a word that may be used pejoratively in common parlance. It conjures images of the unclean outcast, ringing a bell to warn against physical contagion and spiritual pollution and doomed to live out his or her days separated from family, friends, and community.

Leper houses, also known as leper hospitals, were segregated settlements generally consigned to the edge of towns and cities, exerting a physical and psychological effect on the urban landscape, and marking the boundaries of medieval urban society. There were over 300 leper houses in medieval England. Mostly founded between the 12th and 13th centuries, they amounted to nearly a quarter of all hospitals across the country and formed a key element of both the social and religious landscape of the Middle Ages. Warwick leper house was founded by Roger de Beaumont, 2nd Earl of Warwick, in the vicinity of an already existing church towards the end of the reign of Henry 1 of England in about 1135. The warden or head of the leper hospital would have been a priest.

The medieval hospital came into lay hands in 1545 but continued to function as a place of charity and refuge, supporting the sick of the town. In fact, the owner Sir Thomas Puckering is known to have paid half the income of the property to the poor in Warwick. In 1635 he built almshouses beyond the hospital on the Saltisford, where, later in the century, eight women lived supported by £4 each year from the Puckering estate. Between 1702 and 1730, the almshouses were converted to four houses, numbers 112 – 118 Saltisford, and my own great grandmother lived at one time in one of these properties. The properties were however demolished in 1964.

The site is classified by English Heritage as a scheduled monument and the chapel, and the 15th century two storey 'master's House' are both grade II listed buildings. After years of neglect and disrepair, the future of the site has now been secured and, while the history and facade of the site will be preserved, it is likely that the buildings are to be converted into residential dwellings.

It is unsurprising that, much folk lore and strange tales surround the sites of old leper hospitals and the site in Warwick is no exception. During the years of the first World War a solitary young lad aged around twelve, wandered down from his home on the Saltisford one day, seeking adventure in the grounds of the old leper hospital. Only a few hundred yards from his home, the old ruins always fired the imaginations of local children. It was a great place to build a den or have a game of hide and seek.

Michael was fascinated by the decaying old stone and wooden structure with which he had a particularly childlike affinity due to the chapel bearing his name. Climbing over the perimeter fence in the fading late afternoon, intent on exploring the derelict master's house, he landed awkwardly on the inside of the dark and dusty structure after squeezing through one of the small, glassless, windows. A few old hay bales lay amongst the blocks of ancient stone scattered around the otherwise empty and abandoned building. As his eyes acclimatised to the surroundings, the barren space suddenly became filled by the most offensive and foul odour, Michael finding himself struggling hard not to be overwhelmed by an all-consuming stench of putrid, rotting meat.

As he regained his composure, his curiosity drove him to seek out the origin of the smell, the horrendous miasma growing stronger as he crept silently towards a partially collapsed wall at the far end of the building. As he got closer to the wall, his heart raced faster as he noticed movement through the gaps in the stone. Crawling on hands and knees to the end of the building, Michael peered open mouthed through the aperture in the stone and, to his astonishment, directly before his eyes knelt a circle of people clad in filthy yellow stained gowns. Heads bowed as if in prayer, he noted with horror the afflictions and suffering of each individual, some covered in oozing pustules, others with missing limbs. Stood in front of the figures was a priest, flanked by two large candles. Clad in white, he held a crucifix above the heads of the kneeling group and whispered an incantation. On instruction from the priest, the sick struggled to their feet with a peculiar tinkling noise. Once standing, Michael breathlessly observed the brass bells attached to a rope around each of their necks, the combined ringing of the bells echoing eerily in the stillness of the chamber.

Producing a silver chalice, the group frantically recoiled from the advancing clergyman as he sprinkled liquid from the cup towards them. A terrified, inhuman scream rang through Michael's ears as he was suddenly confronted by a pure white face pressed against the other side of the wall, staring at him, and covered in a mass of living sores. As he fled in a state of pure terror, it wasn't until he reached what felt like the relative safety of outside, that he realised the scream he had heard was in fact his own. His mother was shocked by his appearance as he returned home to the family property, on the Saltisford. Deathly pale and shaking uncontrollably from head-to-toe Michael refused to offer his worried Mum an explanation instead racing straight to his bedroom as soon as he could.

It was many decades later that Michael first spoke of his experience to his grandson, also called Michael, the man who recounted this uncanny tale.

"

The Man with Leprosy
'Unclean, unclean' the leper had to say
and sadly watch the people run away.
But then to Jesus at the mountainside he came
to be healed of all his sickness and his shame.
Wow, did you see what Jesus did ?
He touched the leper from whom they hid.
The Holy One touched this unclean soul.
Took away his shame and made him whole.

Royston Nella

CHAPTER 5

ORBS

Mysterious balls of light known commonly as 'orbs' have been captured on video and camera for as long as the technology to record the phenomenon has existed. The explosion of ghost hunting television programmes since the 1990s have really brought and consolidated orbs in public consciousness though. Observed through the eyes of a paranormal believer, orbs are generally thought to be manifestations of energy, with some people convinced they are physical representations of ghosts or spirits. Those with a more practical disposition will tell you that orbs aren't ghostly at all. In photography, backscatter is an optical phenomenon, where the camera flash reflects dust, water droplets or other particles in the air, resulting in circular shapes being captured on an image. It commonly occurs in digital photography in low-light scenes. Looking at photographs of this phenomenon it's easy to conclude that orb happenings can be easily and scientifically explained away. Some orb sightings aren't in low light conditions though and reports of sightings with the naked eye tend to suggest they are solid, without the spokes of light that you would see from backscatter.

Some claim that the orbs they have seen appear to generate their own light. In such instances perhaps there is still a natural explanation for such luminescence. Fireflies are not known to exist in the UK but are common elsewhere around the world. In Britain glow-worms can provide their own subdued light show though.

If we indulge in the esoteric, psychics and spiritualists have claimed to see orbs within an individual's aura and even make claim to different coloured orbs having different meanings. Although the common orbs are transparent or clear, an orb that appears white or silver is said to transmit positive energy. Red or orange orbs are warm or positive spirits, whilst black orbs with a brown or dark hue have a reputation for being negative and attached to angry spirits. Green orbs are always thought to be associated with nature and blue ones with calm and healing. Some say orbs are in fact a separate form of energy that we don't yet have an explanation for. They might be closest to the correct answer.

Orb sightings are often made or captured in predictable places like churches and graveyards. However, this is not always the case. During a visit to Warwick Castle a Dutch tourist claimed to have seen a ghostly mist and strange lights in the grounds one dark December afternoon in 2009. A photograph of the phenomena appeared to show some kind of swirling manifestation along with several orbs of light. The subsequent publication of the picture under the heading ' I saw a ghost at Warwick Castle' attracted a lot of public interest. Some suggested the image captured a cluster of spiritual orbs surrounding a spectral mist, in the process of taking the form of an apparition. Others disagreed stating the misty manifestation was more likely due to the exceptionally cold weather, with cigarette smoke lingering in the freezing air. The orbs possibly being caused by the flash of the camera reflecting off raindrops and snowflakes. Whatever the truth, it's an impressive and evocative photograph.

❧

The long-time owners of a red brick Victorian property set back off the Birmingham Road on the outskirts of Warwick have had some fascinating experiences over many years, most of which have occurred in the large orchard at the rear of their property. The orchard which leads down to the Grand Union canal has, by the admission of its now elderly owners, been allowed to fall into a 'very unkept state'. The vast neglected sprawl is of mainly old fruit trees. Their gnarled boughs intertwine in a weird, chaotic way, rather like a bunch of pipe cleaners. Rotting fruit lies all around with a myriad of insect life filling the air. The scene is a bit depressing as this must have been a beautiful orchard at one time. At the far end of the neglected grounds, you can just make out through the brambles and completely overgrown hedgerow shadows of passersby on the canal towpath and the occasional barge chugging by.

The owners claim to have regularly seen the figure of a stout man amongst the trees as have two generations of the family before them. Dressed in a type of smock tied at the waist, the apparition appears very real on the occasions that it manifests. A floppy battered straw hat adorns his head, and he carries a small scythe like implement. On being approached the figure has been known to turn and give a toothless grimace before melting away into nothingness, giving the impression that it is aware of and interacting with the physical world. The occupants and their family have always known him as 'Grumpy John'. John is believed to be the name of the original owner of the land in this area.

Even more curious than 'Grumpy John' though is the unexplained phenomena that seems to be quite prolific in this strange neglected semi-rural wilderness. As farfetched as it may seem a regular peculiar activity in the old orchard occurs. One that relates to what one might hesitate to call faeries.

Faeries or fairies have been part of many European cultures for centuries. Believers will tell you that there is a distinct difference between 'faeries' and 'fairies'. Fairies being helpful to humans as they are said to be beautiful, kind, and generous. Whilst faeries are allegedly evil and troublesome creatures. Historians tell us that most mythical and folklore depictions of faerie folk that have come down to us through the ages, can usually be traced back to their most likely historical roots. For example, most nature sprites and faeries are usually seen as being derived from pre-Christian gods and goddesses or from pagan concepts of water and tree spirits. In medieval times it was thought that faeries were creatures made from the elements — earth, air, fire, and water. Explanations have also in the past been heavily influenced by religious beliefs, with the sightings attributed much like orbs, to the spirits of the dead or even un-baptised babies.

Faeries are often categorised in paranormal circles alongside other anomalous luminosities such as orbs, fire balls, ghost lights and marsh lights, all with varying numbers of believers and varying rational explanations to potentially satisfy many sightings. Perhaps the most famous of all fairy sightings dates to the early 20th century.

The Cottingley Fairies appeared in a series of photographs from 1917, taken by 16-year-old Elsie Wright and 9-year-old Frances Griffiths, two cousins who lived in Cottingley near Bradford. Acclaimed Sherlock Holmes author Sir Arthur Conan Doyle, on seeing the photographs, was so convinced by the authenticity of the images that he used them to illustrate an article he wrote for the Christmas edition of The Strand Magazine in 1920, confident that they provided real and visible evidence of the fairy phenomena. By modern day standards, the images look like obvious fakes and in the 1980s both girls admitted some of the images were faked using cardboard cut outs of fairies. Frances always maintained however that the fifth and final image of the fairies was genuine.

Back among the old Birmingham Road orchard, it is certain that, during daylight hours and particularly in bright sunlight, all kinds of patterns and shadows are bound to dance through the trees. But it is what the occupants report seeing at dusk and during the night that is both curious and perplexing. Small bright balls of light, more typical of orb phenomena rather than fairy phenomena, are often seen in various parts of the orchard. Varying in colour, sometimes the orbs appear singularly and at other times they are seen in clusters. There have been occasions where the owners claim to have been startled by these lights suddenly shooting past them. In other instances, they have felt as though they are almost being observed by these peculiar little manifestations as they have appeared to be moving in a more deliberate and sentient manner in their presence.

One corner of the orchard that lies in a small hollow has always been known by the family as the 'fairy dell'. It is in this area that the most fascinating observations have been made. The luminosities seen here are slightly larger than the other orbs seen in the orchard and appear with less common shape. Witnessed only on particularly dark and stormy nights, children and indeed the current senior members of the family say that some of them look like tadpoles, but others appear to look more like small, winged creatures. Pipistrelle bats maybe, or perhaps, it is just possible that this old orchard on the outskirts of the town is home to Warwick's very own fairies.

"

'From fairies and tempters of the night, guard me, I
beseech you'
'We see a group of Titania's fairies zooming around,
sprinkling dewdrops on the grasses and flowers "orbs" they call these little drops of water or
"fairy favours"

William Shakespeare.

CHAPTER 6

THE CAPE

The Upper and Lower Cape are areas within in the Saltisford Ward of Warwick. Sitting on the canal side in Lower Cape is the historic and well-known pub The Cape of Good Hope. 'The Cape' as it's known locally was originally owned by the Wills and Clark families. It was part of numerous buildings bought by Thomas Young between 1830 – 47 before the property was subsequently passed through marriage, back to the Wills Family, with Thomas Young's daughter marrying John Wills. The pub was subsequently occupied by Ellen (the widow of John Wills' son, George), her second husband (a Mr Neale whom she married in 1904) and their direct descendants. Mr Neale gave his life in the Service of his Country in the First World War, however, after which Ellen took over the licence in its entirety, managing the establishment until its sale to Flower & Co. On its sale to Flower & Co in 1932, the circle was completed, as the Clark family took tenancy of the pub. There is some conjecture as to the origin of the pub name but apart from the obvious (the rocky headland on the Atlantic coast of the Cape Peninsula in South Africa) there appears to be no clear record of the naming. Perhaps the Georgians felt the name somehow appropriate given its proximity to the water and the passing boats and barges.

As well as the pub, the Cape has a famous association with the Donald Healy Motor Company. A range of the world-famous Healey performance cars were produced at the Cape Works, built on the site of an old pig farm between Cape Road and Lock Lane in 1945. These super-fast cars were quick to capture the public imagination as early as 1946. A timed performance on the Italian Como-Milan Autostrata of 106.56 mph drew a Motor Magazine of the day to comment "no other car has been timed at so high a speed". Further successes followed in the Mille Miglia, the Monte Carlo Rally and at Le Mans. Production prototypes were constructed at the Cape Works for the Nash-Healey, Austin Healey 100, 100S, 100-6 and 3000 as well as for the Frogeye and Mark II Sprites. The Cape works also housed production facilities for Healey Marine Boats. Donald Healey regularly socialised at The Cape of Good Hope alongside friends and colleagues. One can only speculate how many ideas for those wonderful cars of yesteryear were discussed over a pint in the pub.

❧

There are numerous tales of ghosts and happening attached to the pub. A long-time previous landlady of the pub was Doris Harrison whose portrait stares somewhat disapprovingly at current day clients from behind the bar. Described as a formidable woman, Doris was renowned for not taking any nonsense from any of her more lively customers. She and her husband ran the pub for many years and some older residents of the town still recall her with some trepidation. Current staff at the pub tell of occasions where glasses left lying around have inexplicably been re stacked neatly behind the bar and there have also been instances of dirty glasses being sent crashing to the floor from shelves and worktops. The poltergeist activity may well have something to do with the legendary Doris and the fastidious way she 'ruled' her establishment.

One of the most active and regularly witnessed by staff and locals is the spectre of a young girl dressed in white. Around seven years of age, she was christened the 'running girl' due to her frantic activity, running at great pace up and down stairs and throughout the premises. It's not clear whether she is in pursuit of something or someone or whether she herself is being pursued by an unseen entity. Somewhat unnervingly and usually during her late-night appearances, her running is sometimes accompanied by screaming too.

Another shadowy female figure is also often seen floating through the rear bar area. Although the apparition appears to shun traditional methods of entering or exiting a room (instead emerging and disappearing through the walls of the bar area), doors do swing open, and slam shut in her wake. Her own image is silent and determined, her gaze remaining focused and forward as she moves along the same route. A vision of the past being played over and over again. To the front of the bar, the apparition of an old-fashioned bargee in grey overalls, a drab baggy jacket and woollen hat has been witnessed, contentedly smoking a briar pipe in flagrant disregard to the smoking ban in pubs.

Another strange phenomenon reported by resident staff staying in the front bedrooms of the pub is an audible rather than visual manifestation. During the night, the sound of coughing or choking is said to emanate from the tow path directly in front of the building. Witnesses describe the sound as very disturbing, as though someone is fighting for their breath. On several occasions staff have gone down to investigate but nothing has ever been seen. The sound has been linked with the passing of Robert Harkell, who died in July 1875.

47-year-old local boatman Harkell had been living in the Saltisford area for around 11 months and was drinking in the bar of the Cape of Good Hope Inn at the end of a Friday working shift. Another local man, Henry Lidgett, who was at the time the temporary employee of the Warwick and Napton Canal Company, was also drinking in the pub. That morning Henry's wife had given him a beefsteak for his lunch and the pub landlord had agreed that he could cook the meat in the oven at the public house. When the meat was cooked and removed from the oven by the landlord, Robert asked if he could try a piece of the succulent roast. The landlord gave him permission to cut off some, and he did so. By now the bar area was full, but no one noticed whether Harkell started to eat the meat in the room.

Robert's wife had been waiting at home for some time but, as usual, his time at the pub had become extended and he was late for the evening supper that had been prepared for him.

In a rage she set of to the tavern to frog march her husband back home. As she approached the pub, she saw Robert standing outside talking to another man, and shortly afterwards he turned from her and went back into the tavern. She stopped briefly to talk and complain about Robert to a neighbour who was drinking on the canal bank before setting back on her mission to retrieve him. When she went towards the door of the public house, she was greeted by the sight of her husband in the passage, advancing towards her seemingly trying to vomit. Exiting the pub, Harkell stumbled to a stile adjoining the premises. His wife noticed that he continued to make efforts to vomit, and that his neck and ear had both become very dark and swollen in appearance. Becoming alarmed, she ran to the public house door, and calling to Henry Lidgett, said, "Oh, good God, run Harry, our Bob's dying". Shortly afterwards she became hysterical.

Henry ran to the spot and found 'Bob' lying on the ground with his face downwards. With difficulty he lifted him up, and looking in his face, declared to the assembled crowd, "He's quite dead; he's quite dead". Robert Harkell lay unconsciousness and totally motionless and Henry remained with him until a surgeon by the name of Mr J R Nunn was summoned. The doctor could find no pulse on the unfortunate man. At the subsequent postmortem examination Mr Nunn said that he had found a piece of beef, two and a half inches long and one inch thick, lodged in Harkell's gullet. At the inquest at The Black Horse Inn, Saltisford, Warwick, Mr G Moore, borough coroner, reported that the boatman had accidentally suffocated in his attempts to swallow a piece of meat.

❧

On 3rd December 1887 an inquest was held at the Cape of Good Hope Inn on the body of William Wellington of number 11 the Packmores. Wellington was found drowned in the canal the same morning. The foreman of the jury on that day knew Mr Wellington very well and described him as being permanently depressed on account of his poor eyesight being blind in one eye. He also suffered badly with sciatica which led him to walk with an extremely pronounced limp. A local man called Richard Blaham recalled that at about a quarter to eight on the morning in question he was walking along the canal in front of the Cape of Good Hope Inn when he saw Mr Wellington walking on the opposite side of the canal. He was walking nervously up and down near the locks when Mr Blaham first saw him. Another person also saw Mr Wellington about twenty minutes later in a similarly agitated state.

Mr Samuel Reynolds, landlord of the Cape of Good Hope Inn, said he had known William Wellington all his life but unfortunately his disabilities had led him to become a heavy drinker. Mr Reynolds had also seen William that day at about a quarter to eight in the morning, near the lock, pacing backwards and forwards. At about ten minutes past eight Mr Reynolds had heard a boatman shouting for help and immediately ran out and found Mr Wellington seemingly standing upright in the water at the mouth of the lock with just his head visible. The lock itself was empty and after a struggle he managed to drag Mr Wellington out of the water and immediately sent for a police-constable.

When local officer PC Salt arrived at the scene, he found Mr Wellington lying on the towing path and immediately pronounced him deceased despite his body still being warm. He could find no marks of violence on the body, nor anything in his possession. With the assistance of Mr Reynolds he took the body to the Cape of Good Hope Inn. The coroner presiding over the inquest briefly addressed the jury, and pointed out that, in his opinion, the evidence adduced could only justify a verdict of "found drowned". After a few minutes' consideration, the jury returned a verdict in accordance with the coroner's view.

Most reports of sightings of apparitions or ghosts occur during the dark hours. There are historical claims in this instance however, of a mysterious eye patch wearing, limping man seen in the early morning all throughout the year. He steps into the canal from the bank opposite the Cape of Good Hope, walking deeper into its depths before disappearing entirely. No traces of the man have ever been found.

"

'And as to being in a fright,
Allow me to remark
That ghosts have just as good a right, In every way, to
fear the light,
As men to fear the dark.

Lewis Carroll — 'Phantasmagoria' 1869.

A curious little story is told by a couple living in the Cape area of Warwick which concerns their 7-year-old daughter. Chloe is an exceptionally bright, well-adjusted little girl with a delightful demeanour and engaging personality. Mum and dad are a professional couple in their late thirties and have become increasingly perplexed by the extraordinary and detailed accounts relayed to them by their daughter.

Whist it is quite common for children of this age to have an imaginary friend, Chloe, an only child, has since a very young age, consistently referred to her 'previous life' and the characters and experiences associated with it. Usually regarded as a phase which the child quickly grows out of, in Chloe's case this shows no sign of abating.

In her previous life Chloe says her name was Ella and her parents were called Simon and Ruth (notably not her real parents' names). She makes these claims with such conviction and certainty that her parents say they are reticent to challenge her. From the detail she gives of the clothing both she and her 'parents' wore, it seems her recollections likely relate to the late Victorian period. Pictures she has drawn of herself, and her previous parents do indeed, somewhat surprisingly, capture images from that era. It is known that between the ages of three to nine, children do report dreams which can be lucid and complex. By the ages of five to seven their dreams can take on a 'movie like' quality with the dreamers themselves actively participating as characters. In Chloe's case however, her experiences always appear to take place during waking hours so cannot be attributed to dreams. In her bedroom Chloe is regularly overheard in conversation with people she claims visit her. According to her parents the dialogue is always rational and eerily pertinent to everyday Victorian life.

Chloe has also spoken of how she likes to attend the church close to the family home, along with her parents Simon and Ruth and other friends from the local congregation. There is no church close to the family home, nor has she ever regularly attended church services with her family. There was once however, a small chapel constructed of corrugated steel not far from the current family home. Known locally as 'The Tabernacle' it stood 50 yards from the Cape of Good Hope pub. The building had been owned by St. Marys church and was used as a mission room then later as a foundry. The building has long since been demolished but just maybe this is the place of worship that Chloe refers to.

Reincarnation is the theory that the non-physical essence of a living being (often referred to as the soul), will begin a new life in a different form or body after the occurrence of biological death. It's certainly not a new concept and forms the central tenet of many religions including Buddhism, Hinduism, Jainism and Sikhism. Although definitions of the term paranormal vary greatly, most definitions would consider that evidence relating to the possibility of reincarnation is well within the remit of parapsychology. The concept has been greatly debated by philosophers away from religion too and has even been studied in scientific circles. Psychiatrist Ian Stevenson, who died in 2007, undertook a large amount of study on the subject from the 1960s onwards and is known to have interviewed over 3000 children globally on the subject. While cautious to conclude that his studies provided conclusive evidence of reincarnation, he did determine that many characteristics exhibited or experiences reported by children, were difficult to attribute to genetics and their environment alone. He published a book in 1966, titled and detailing 'Twenty Cases Suggestive of Reincarnation'. Even more evocative is his 1997 work 'Reincarnation and Biology: A Contribution to the Ethilogy of Birthmarks and Birth Defects' in which he details two hundred reported cases where birthmarks or defects all in some way correspond with wounds or injuries that a child recalled incurring in a past life.

Many other scientists and researchers of course, typically approach claims around reincarnation with extreme caution, often looking for naturalistic explanation before siding with the extraordinary. The case of little Chloe recalling with such clarity, precise details of her 'previous life' and of those she claims to have shared it with nonetheless remains fascinating, and more than a little spooky.

CHAPTER 7

RETURN TO JURY STREET (PART 1)

_____

During my first foray into investigating the strange happenings in and around Jury Street, I encountered tales of ghostly happenings in pubs and restaurants, haunted houses and the mystery surrounding the Warwick tunnels. Since publishing Whispers from Warwick, even more tales have come to my attention, centred around what must be a leading candidate for the title of the most haunted street in Warwick. In 1916 it was the scene of a dramatic tram accident when a driverless tram left its station outside the Warwick Arms Hotel and careered the full length of the street and left the rails at the East Gate and crashed into the Castle Arms pub injuring three. Like passengers on that early 20th century tram, so we now hurtle together into further unexplained happenings on Jury Street.

The East Gate is one of the two remaining medieval gates to the town and stands at the eastern end of Jury Street at its meeting place with Smith Street, Castle Hill and The Butts. The gateway was built in the 14th century. In 1426 the chapel of St Peter was added over the arch. By 1576 the chapel was falling into decay and was acquired by Warwick Corporation for education purposes. Until 1590 it was occupied by the King's Grammar School. Later it became The King's High School for girls. From modest beginnings in 1879 the girls school operated from its Smith Street/Eastgate site for 140 years until its move to Myton Road. There are rumours that the original site was haunted by two young girls, dressed in tunic dresses, with pinafores and blouses. Uniform typical for 19th century schoolgirls.

The poet Walter Savage Landor was born at Eastgate House, (now known as Landor House). Above the door to Landor House the words 'Landor born 1775' can be read and this building too was once used by The King's High School for girls. Landor was a close friend to Charles Dickens and godfather to his second son, Walter Savage Landor Dickens. There have been suggestions over the years that Landor House too is haunted. Perhaps it is the ghost of Walter himself. He 'loved the light airy house at the top of Smith Street' which was the Landor family home for over 80 years and once wrote of it:

'Never without a pang do I leave the house where I was born'.

It is around the structure of the Eastgate that claims of the vision of a cleric have also been seen. Clad in medieval robes, some say he looks to the heavens, others say he kneels in prayer, but all report him to be wearing an expression of extreme angst. Some have suggested this could be the ghost of English Roman Catholic Priest John Sugar (or Suker).

Sugar was ordained a priest from the English College in Doui France in 1601 and sent on a mission in that year. He was arrested just outside Warwick at Rowington on the 8th July 1603 along with another local man called Robert Grissold. He was not accused of any specific act of treason, but simply of acting as a priest in England, contrary to the Jesuits, etc Act of 1584. After a year in prison at Warwick Sugar and Grissold were condemned on 14th July 1604 to be hanged drawn and quartered, Sugar for being a priest and Grissold for assisting him.

Sugar suffered a horrendous end being cut down and dismembered before he was fully dead. It is said he endured his fearful death with 'exemplary courage'. His recorded words during the ordeal nothing less than poetic:

'I shall soon be above the sun' and 'after a sharp dinner I shall have a sweet supper'.

Sugar and his companion were beatified on 22nd November 1987 by Pope John Paul II. Their feast day is every 16th July. Along with William Freeman (also hung drawn and quartered at Warwick on 13th August 1595) the three are known as The Warwick Martyrs. There is a painting by the artist Rebecca Dering depicting Sugar before his execution. Interestingly the building in the background resembles very closely a property which still stands in Jury Street.

❧

Crossing The Butts into Jury Street the first property you encounter on the right is number 37. This magnificent grade II listed building was originally built in the 16/17th century. However apart from the 17th Century carved panel above the door no original exterior work can be seen. The front is facsimile timber framing in keeping with the town probably constructed in the mid-1800s. The rainwater head is dated 1856.

This property was the home of Dr James Cooke who was a surgeon and writer during the time of the English Civil War. Dr Cooke founded the Baptist Chapel on Castle Hill and became pastor there in 1670. He was a surgeon of considerable repute publishing a famous book on surgery and was appointed physician to the Earl of Warwick. Dr Cooke died in 1688 and is buried at St Mary's Church.

Dr Cooke was a friend of the physician John Hall the son in law of William Shakespeare. After Hall's death, Cooke purchased two of his books on case notes and translated them from Latin. The books were published in 1657. A local psychic medium who contacted me, claims to have seen the shadows of two men wearing tricorn hats in one of the bay windows of the house, poring over some ancient volume. Perhaps this is the two physicians, still musing together through the entries in Hall's book, 'Select observations on English bodies: or, Cures both empericall and historicall performed upon very eminent persons in desperate diseases'.

For many years outside numbers 33 to 35 Jury Street has hung an old iron vessel from which this ancient property took its name, 'The Porridge Pot'. The name refers to a massive similarly shaped pot in the Great Hall at Warwick Castle which belonged to Guy Earl of Warwick in the 11th century. This building is a medieval structure with a facade dating from 1700 with the lower storey having two 18th century shop type windows each having a half-glazed door. There is a third original 6 - fielded-panelled door on the extreme right-hand side.

Several years ago, the name was transferred to a new business at Longbridge and the Jury Street building became a Pizza Express restaurant. Almost immediately staff at the renamed restaurant reported seeing a ghostly figure at the top of the cellar steps at the front of the building. The manager became so concerned at these sightings that, for a while he closed off access to the cellar. When questioned about what or who they had seen, each witness described a man in a long coat wearing a tall top hat. There is a well published photograph from the 1850s capturing the image of a woman and a man deep in conversation by the door to this property. She is standing on the step, hands on hips, wearing a pinafore over a long dress. The gentleman wears a frock coat with a high starched collar and wearing a tall top hat. His identity currently remains a mystery, but he presumably retains a very deep affinity with the place.

There is still plenty of paranormal activity regularly occurring at the old Porridge Pot. At the rear of the building there used to be a balcony accessed by stairs at either end. A very pale woman in a long white robe is often seen by staff, floating from side to side high above the room where the balcony would have been. The vision is said to be particularly clear when the sun shines through the window behind. The ambience of the restaurant and the building itself is full of character and makes for a delightful dining experience. Members of staff, however, have reported that a less comfortable atmosphere can pervade at closing time when the property is empty of diners and other colleagues. The task of locking up is seemingly not a desirable one. One of the longer serving ladies says even when she is certain that the place is empty, there is still a most peculiar sensation of something or someone loitering behind the front door, as if waiting for the key to turn in order that nocturnal happenings can commence.

❧

Redfern House stands at number 29 Jury Street. It has an imposing frontage reached by wide stone steps from the pavement. It has an impressive front door above which sits a semicircular panel inlaid with stained glass which displays the name Redfern. In recent years this has been the registered address of several different companies. However, it's most famous for being the home and shop of Charles Redfern (c1798–1868) who in the 1840s and 50s was probably the most well-known dealer in antiques and curiosities outside of London.

During the early part of the 19th Century buying historical objects and curios became an important aspect of fashionable taste, furnishing and the evolving culture of collecting. A market in historical objects was created and sustained throughout Britain by an emerging class of dealers. Antiquarian publications, practical manuals on historic architecture and romantic fiction were amongst some of the most sought-after items amongst an increasing number of avid collectors. Charles Redfern acted as an agent for collectors being a purchaser at high profile auction disposals and spent much of his time every year searching the continent for material. He was the proprietor of the shop at his home in Jury Street. In the Directory of Warwick for 1850 his business was promoted as 'one of the best and most expensive curiosity shops ... full of antiques and old objects whose multitude and variety could not be exceeded in any collection in London'.

Famous American writer Nathaniel Hawthorne (1804–1864), came to Warwick in 1862 and wrote a detailed account of his visit, recorded in his memoir 'Our Old Home: A series of English Sketches'. In his account 'About Warwick', Hawthorne noted:

'If the visitor is inclined to carry away any little memorial of Warwick, he had better go to an old Curiosity Shop in Jury Street where there is a vast quantity of obsolete gewgaws, great and small, and many of them so pretty and ingenious that you wonder how they came to be thrown aside and forgotten. The shop in question is near the East Gate but is hardly to be found without careful search, being denoted only by the name 'REDFERN' painted not very conspicuously in the top light of the door. Immediately on entering we find ourselves among a confusion of old rubbish and valuables, ancient armour, historic portraits, ebony cabinets, tall ghostly clocks, and hideous old china'.

What is perhaps less well known about this prolific writer is that he had an abiding interest in the supernatural and some of his finest works were his ghost stories. It is said that Hawthorne was haunted by a paranormal presence that accompanied him wherever he went throughout his life. The identity of his ghostly accomplice was however, never revealed in any of his writings or literature and remains a mystery. So strong was this presence that it is claimed by some that the 'Hawthorne ghost' not only still lurks around his birthplace in Massachusetts but in several other significant buildings that Hawthorne visited during his life. This may account for speculation that Redfern House is haunted by an unidentified ghost. Maybe Hawthorn's tortured soul left a legacy at this curious old Warwick residence.

"

'Along the smooth gleam and shadow of the quiet stream, through a vista of willows that droop on either side into the water, we behold the grey magnificence of Warwick Castle, uplifting itself among stately trees, and rearing its turrets high above their lofty branches'

Nathaniel Hawthorne 1862

CHAPTER 8

VICTORIANS

Peter epitomises the very definition of a true English gentlemen. Now an octogenarian Peter was born in Warwick Hospital in 1941 and apart from military service is a lifelong resident of the town. His affinity and love for his hometown is deep and passionate. His phenomenal powers of recollection suggest an almost a photographic memory which makes him a most charming and engaging individual. So vivid are his memories that you feel you have almost experienced them yourself after chatting with him. He spent his early childhood living above the well-known shoe shop in Warwick's Coten End. Originally Wridgways boot and shoe shop, it was known for many years by locals as the Clark's shop, before becoming Charles Clinkards shoes.

Over the years thousands of schoolchildren in the town have had their feet measured for the 'sensible' school shoes we either loved, or perhaps more often, hated. No 'winkle pickers' for school for the children of the 50s and 60s. Just good, stout boring shoes that would take all the rigours of the school playground. Although raised by his parents in strict, typical for the era fashion, Peter recalls with impish schoolboy humour how he and his pals would get maximum value from their weekly pocket money when attending the Warwick cinema opposite his home, hiding behind their seats after the conclusion of the Saturday matinee to rewatch the film on its second showing!

Peter maintains that even in the early days of his childhood he was always aware of a sense of presence around him. Of notable interest is that fact that he is also a twin. Although Peter himself doesn't relate his experiences directly to being a twin, general interest TV programs and articles still regularly arise around the subject of twins, often relating to some sensational, inexplicable happening. In many West African nations, deep rooted cultural beliefs still prevail that twins have supernatural abilities and can communicate with spirits and ancestors in ways that, ordinarily people cannot. Peter has had several unexplained experiences during his long life, but one phenomenon remains clearly etched in his memory to this very day. While there was no way that Peter would ever be able to engage either of his parents in his thoughts and experiences for fear of their predictable reaction, his twin sister did share some of his experiences. The Paradise Street phenomena was certainly one of them.

In 1952 the family moved to a property in Paradise Street in Warwick. A row of unremarkable Victorian Terraced houses that even in modern times still provide well built, solid traditional family accommodation. Shortly after moving to their new home Peter observed regular fleeting glimpses of what he initially thought was his aunt, who lived locally, passing the house. After a while he realised it was not his aunt, but a middle-aged woman unknown to him, with a somewhat seemingly haughty disposition. Although well-dressed, her outfit comprised of dark, Victorian style clothes, notably out of keeping with what others were wearing, even to an 11-year-old boy. The long skirt, giving the appearance that she would preternaturally 'glide' rather than walk past the house before quickly disappearing out of sight. Peter's sister said she had also seen the woman who began to appear more frequently, but at the rear of the property rather than the front of it. The twins both caught the lady peering through back windows on numerous occasions, after which she would simply turn her back, glide down the garden and fade away. Understandably frightened by the regular appearance of the apparition, the children felt they could only ever confide in one another until many years later, their mother too spoke of seeing the phantom of a Victorian lady on numerous occasions. The wooden name plaque carved by Peter's father is still in place on the wall of the house and each time Peter passes the property his vivid memories come flooding back. He is noncommittal as to whether he still sees the Victorian lady in the area though.

It is a curiosity that, a hugely disproportionate number of ghost sightings are of individuals from the Victorian era, when it spans only 63 years of approximately 300,000 years of human existence. There are rarely, if ever reports of seeing the ghosts of neanderthals. But more than any generation before them, the Victorians were drawn to, and some might say obsessed with the afterlife.

The subject of the paranormal was of intense interest. The Victorians created many parlour and mirror games some of which still exist today in certain communities. Ghost stories flourished and were voraciously devoured by readers. Seances made for acceptable entertainment at dinner parties, and, at the other end of the societal spectrum, the notion of ghosts was subjected to serious scientific and philosophical scrutiny. This was no doubt motivated in no small part by the very common presence of death in Victorian Britain.

Many children died very young. The death of mothers in childbirth was still common and mundane activities such as day-to-day travel and work, would result in unexpected accidents, often with fatal consequences. This seems to have been the genesis for the idea that ghosts are the spirits of individuals who lost their lives too soon. While the subject of death is almost taboo in modern Britain, it seems that the Victorians were so entrenched in it, that they almost embraced it. The practice of cutting of locks of hair of the dead for keepsakes, and rules around the wearing of 'mourning' colours were all established during the Victorian era. While some of these practices still endure today, the practice of postmortem photography has fallen by the wayside. Families would commonly pose for a final picture with a lost loved one, and while this no doubt bought solace to families of the era, both the concept and the photographs that can be easily found, would be extremely disturbing to many in the modern era.

Ultimately, we can fall on several explanations as to why we seem to see more ghostly Victorians. There may be something of a scientific explanation. The spirits of those who have passed may exist within a visible realm for only a finite time, deteriorating until they are no longer observable by humans. It may be that in reality, ghosts exist only in our heads, with the concept remaining alive in society as a gift from our Victorian ancestors with which we inextricably but possibly unconsciously link the two. Or maybe, something was discovered by those scientists who first credibly studied ghosts and the afterlife. Is it possible they discovered something that no generation before them had discovered and many from Victorian society still walk the earth in reward of their endeavours?

CHAPTER 9

RETURN TO JURY STREET (PART 2)

The properties that were once numbers 4 to 6 Jury Street, are currently known as Ronnie's Bar. Entering the premises, you could easily imagine you had wandered into some up market London emporium. The live music stage areas, Japanese conservatory and décor are de rigueur, but the old Warwick building refuses to be transformed totally. It's twisting rooms and nooks and crannies are a giveaway that this place has significant history. The modern happening scene is almost entirely contained within the ground floor area and whilst the chic clientele enjoys the ambience, the cellars and upper rooms retain an entirely different feel.

The current occupants of the premises have made the private living quarters in the upper rooms very much their own. Original wooden staircases, uneven floors and odd shaped rooms have been furnished and decorated in quite an eclectic manner. Beautiful paintings adorn the walls, some of them depicting the occupants' ancestors. Other paintings offer a reminder of the South of France from which area the lady of the house hails. The French theme is enhanced by exquisite period furniture which sits beneath the old English beams. A framed letter from Sir Winston Churchill hangs on the wall along with other intriguing artefacts and memorabilia. All of this serves to enhance a somewhat haunting atmosphere in a building where the old and the new sit a little awkwardly side by side.

Over the years the property has served many purposes. Number 4 had for many years been a tea rooms and more lately an Italian restaurant. A faded, but still legible, direction sign at the foot of the staircase leading from the ground floor informs that the firm of Horton and Sons Solicitors, once occupied the upper rooms. The corridor on the first floor, would have at one time led to rooms used as offices by the lawyers. At the end of the corridor now, is a bricked-up archway which would have linked this part of the building to Pageant House and the Court House further along the street.

Unexplained happenings have occurred along the top corridor in the two adjoining rooms. Alongside a local paranormal investigator/ spirit medium, I was generously afforded the opportunity to explore and investigate the entire property as I undertook research for this book. The corridor itself is an area where staff have always felt uneasy and the investigator with me claimed that there was a distinct male presence restlessly lurking here, although it is unclear who this character might be. On the walls of one of the tired and sparsely furnished old rooms adjoining the corridor, sits a couple of old paintings one of which appears to be a poignant reminder of who once possibly worked in this part of the building. It is by the artist E. Barrie and is titled 'The Solicitor'. It depicts an elderly austere looking gentleman clad in formal attire, staring wistfully back at anyone who cares to view his portrait.

The room offers an excellent vantage point from which to wave off clients and revellers as they pour out onto Jury Street at the end of the evening. On several occasions the vision of a tall gentleman adorning a long coat and high collar has been seen stood behind staff. Some accounts suggest he has long grey hair while others suggest that he is wearing a wig. Given the properties history, some have suggested that it could be the ghost of Mr Horton, the solicitor who once practiced in the very same room.

The cellars are as you would anticipate in such an old building. Steeply descending worn sandstone steps lead to an ancient wooden door with mysterious diamond shaped patterns cut into it. Beyond this are numerous alcoves and stone shelving all under barrel vaulted ceilings. There is a somewhat out of place set of what appear to be horse troughs. With no obvious modern access to the area for horses one can only conclude that at some point in the past, draymen were able to lead their beasts to this area for refreshment. Some staff have described the atmosphere in this area as creepy and oppressive, and others have felt a sensation of being watched. During our visit, the paranormal investigator suggested that the angry spirit of a previously employed young man with an axe to grind, loiters in this space.

The question as to why the bar is named 'Ronnies', is often asked. Many celebrities who share the name are commemorated in the bar. Tributes to many of them adorn the walls with portraits and autographs on show. The Ronnie in question, however, was a very famous (or some might claim infamous) sculptor. Lord Ronald Charles Sutherland-Leveson-Gower who was born in 1845 and died in 1916. One assumes that for ease of reference, on account of his somewhat grandiose title, he acquired the sobriquet 'Ronnie'.

Born on 2nd August 1845, Lord Ronald Charles Sutherland-Leveson-Gower was the youngest of the eleven children of the 2nd Duke of Sutherland. His childhood was spent at the family homes of Cliveden, Dunrobin and Stafford House. He was educated at Eton, which he disliked, and at Trinity College Cambridge, which he adored but left without completing a degree. Although he was the Liberal MP for Sutherland between 1867 and 1874, he had no heart for the work and spoke in Parliament only once. His interests lay in the world of art and letters.

He trained as a sculptor and published several monographs of British Artists as well as histories of the Tower of London, Joan of Arc and the last days of Marie Antionette. He was also a trustee of the National Portrait Gallery and the Shakespeare Memorial Building at Stratford Upon Avon which drew him often to the area. In 1883 he published a volume of old reminiscences and in 1902 he published his Old Diaries. A friend of Oscar Wilde, many have suggested that the character of Lord Henry Wootton in Wilde's The Picture of Dorian Gray (1890), was based on 'Ronnie'. Gower's most famous sculpture is the Shakespeare monument situated in the neighbouring town of Stratford Upon Avon and Oscar Wilde spoke at the unveiling of the monument on 10th October 1888.

Wilde also recited the following sonnet by Mrs R.S. De Courcy Laffan, wife of the local grammar school's headmaster in tribute to Lord Gower at the unveiling:

> Aye so, methinks, by the red embers' glare,
> Silent he sat, with eagle eyes astrain,
> And saw the myriad children of his brain
> Take form and semblance on the midnight air:
> Heard Royal Henry chide his self-crowned heir,
> The guilty Queen moan for her hand's white stain,
> Or Falstaff troll some roystering refrain,
> Or Hamlet play with his own soul's despair,
> And as the soul thrilled to their changing tone
> Thy hand, O Sculptor, in that hour supreme,
> Smote with swift strokes his being into stone.
> We, too, have dreamt beside our Avon's stream
> Of this great haunting presence – though alone
> Could'st give it substance worthy of our dream!

Rumour has it that Gower was a regular visitor to the Jury Street house, and many believe that his spirit continues to reside in the building, roaming the first-floor rooms and keeping a careful eye on proceedings. He was quite a character by all accounts. A man with boundless energy and deep affection for many things and people. His perfection as a host, his generosity, unselfishness, and his great desire that all about him should be happy rendered him very special to friends and acquaintances alike. The team at modern Ronnies like to think they replicate his gregarious character within their own.

❧

A further tale from Jury Street at its junction with The Butts and Eastgate at the top of Castle Hill comes from a local musician. I first became acquainted with Rich when asking for permission to publish the lyrics to 'The Ballad of Bendigo Mitchell' by the 'Wychwood Folk-Rock band' in Whispers from Warwick (capturing as they do, the story of Bendigo Mitchell so evocatively). *Everyone has a ghost story* and Rich has kindly shared his with me.

The old Warwick fire station was once situated behind a stone wall, in a courtyard that sat adjacent to another large house. The large house was next to the exit from the walk-way known locally as the tink-a-tank and the Ashton family occupied this property for many years. An engine house stood in the yard in which two appliances were housed. Older residents of the town may remember that a large pole was located near the entrance to the fire station, on top of which was mounted a siren, activated whenever need arose to call retained fire fighters to duty. More than likely an air raid siren used in the second world war, it was an eerie sound that could be heard for miles around.

Alongside the fire station, set back from the road behind part of the original town wall sat a small two storey building which was used as a workshop by Rich's grandfather Alec and his colleague Mr Sutton. The two gentlemen were employed by the then Warwick Borough Council. Alec was a signwriter, a real craftsman of his day. He painted amongst other things the entrance signs that would welcome you as you entered the ancient town. He would also use his skills in painting and lettering any other signs or municipal vehicles owned by the local authority. Such was his reputation Alec was employed by many businesses that required shop signs or awning signs written. Old photographs of the town will show many shops and commercial premises displaying signs that were painted by his hand. Unfortunately, such craftsmen and their skills have been lost to the age of the computer and digital printing. Alec passed away following a stroke in the mid-1960s. Mr Sutton was a carpenter, another craftsman of that time and Rich still has a pair of wooden step ladders that Mr Sutton made for his grandfather. A very precious memento of a bye gone era.

Back in the early 1980s, Rich was working at Frederick Freer, a canvas goods and marquee hire business located at 78 West Street Warwick. Born in 1875, Frederick was known as Warwick's master tent maker. He originally started his business at his parents' house at 44 Smith Street before moving in 1944 to the West Street premises. After finishing work that day Rich was walking home to Emscote Road down Jury Street and approaching the Eastgate Arch at the top of Smith Street. It was still sunny and warm, and he recalls that the clock face on St Peter's Chapel above the arch had recently been renovated. In the late afternoon sun, the numerals on the dial shone gold against the brilliant blue background. Just after passing the hanging cauldron above what was then The Porridge Pot tea rooms, he was suddenly overcome with a sensation that to this day he finds incredibly hard to articulate, even with his own ability to convey vivid stories and emotion through lyrics and song. The strange feelings were inextricably attached to the image of an elderly gentleman approaching from the opposite direction, walking up the hill in the direction of the town centre. As the man grew closer, Rich to his astonishment immediately recognised him. It was unmistakably his late grandfather Alec.

Rich recalls with total clarity that the gentleman caught his eye as he walked past and smiled knowingly. The vision was accompanied by very faint, but instantly recognisable odours of acid drops and turpentine, smells strongly associated with his childhood memories of his late grandfather. Momentarily rooted to the spot he gathered his thoughts for the briefest of moments and turned on his heels. The vision of his grandfather was suddenly nowhere to be seen, nor was there any other similar figure walking gently back up the hill. The experience left Rich with an overwhelming feeling of warmth, comfort, and calm. The brief reappearance of his grandfather reassuring, as if to relay the sentiment that, 'it's alright'.

The incident happened over 40 years ago, and Rich has not had any further encounters with his grandfather, nor has he witnessed any similar apparitions. He is emphatic about the strange incident though and continues to derive great solace from the comforting, warm and reassuring sensation that has continued to accompany him ever since that day. He has recalled his tale in a song called 'Lately' which is about his personal memories growing up in Warwick.

"

Lately

On Jury Street one sunny day
I saw a ghost ... it was OK
He just smiled and walked away
Many years after he'd died
Grandad Elbourne painted signs
Around the town, vans and blinds

Left me feeling warm and fine
Smelled of acid drops and turpentine
Lately I've been wandering 'round
The streets and places of my hometown
Seeing what's been put up and what's pulled down
Memories of my hometown

CHAPTER 10

THEATRE STREET

The grade II listed Globe Hotel stands at the corner of Theatre Street in the heart of Warwick and has been a popular hostelry with locals and visitors to the town for many years. It was first opened in 1788 as the Globe Inn Commercial and Posting House. A posting house (or post house) was usually an ale house or inn where horses were kept and could be rented or charged out. Only major towns had post houses, signifying the historic prestige of Warwick. Postriders would sometimes be used to deliver mail and parcels, operating as the post offices of their era. Postilions or post boys were individuals who could also be hired to assist coachmen on their journeys. Riders and horses could also be hired to transport travellers by carriage or coach, stopping at various destinations according to a schedule, much like today's modern transport timetables. Such routes were known as post roads.

In the early 1800s the building became a theatre hosting pantomime and plays characterised by irreverent and bawdy humour of the era. However, unlike it's rather more famous neighbour at nearby Stratford Upon Avon, the Warwick theatre only operated for a relatively short time. An iron bridge, constructed in 1804, once spanned the medieval Holloway, facilitating access until the 1960s.

Having housed a popular Thai restaurant for many years and watering holes under other names, the property reverted to its original historic name in 2015, being reinvented as a charming contemporary boutique hotel and gastropub with an extensive menu serving traditional dishes along with Mediterranean food and pizzas.

Despite the plush refurbishment, a distinct feeling of time standing still will meet anybody descending into the cellar areas. Narrow, steep stone stairs lead to a dank and dark labyrinth of tiny corridors and doors that reek history. Alongside the barrel-vaulted ceilings, small alcoves and ancient iron rods protruding from weathered walls, sudden and variable drops in temperature leave you feeling as uneasy as you feel in awe. There are narrow accesses to little courtyards below the building and the walls they are encased in vary, from Victorian red brick to sandstone blocks. No two of these small areas are alike adding a sense of peculiarity. In an environment tailor made to play tricks with your mind, it is surprising not to find stories of high strangeness here.

Retaining much of its historic features, the original stairs lead to the guest rooms on the upper floors, where modern décor and features are blended around a quirky configuration of rambling rooms, nooks, and crannies. Most of the upstairs rooms have sloping floors and period sash windows. The wooden panelling in the rooms gives a clear insight into the buildings 18th century post house past and some small stained-glass panels provide additional character. It is from rooms nine and ten that some eerie experiences have been reported by guests.

Room nine was originally kept as a banqueting room where the great and the good of the town would feast in the 18th century. The modern-day room is indeed quite lavishly decorated, a four-poster bed adding to its opulent charm. Shadowy figures and the sounds of merry making are said to have awoken and unsettled several past guests, resulting in early hour relocation requests (despite odd activities always abating quickly). Guests in room 10 are known to have reported similarly strange occurrences during the night, including sudden and rapid drops in temperature, again accompanied by unexplained shadows. The sightings of spectres are not confined solely to the hotel. From an upstairs window, standing in the doorway of number 33 Theatre Street opposite the hotel, a little girl dressed in a white smock and bonnet has been before vanishing.

Although the modern day, rather fashionable look of this old three storey coaching Inn is quite beguiling, it belies the uncommonness within its ancient walls. Those with an appetite for a night with the unexplained might like to book a room for themselves. If you're feeling brave, be sure to ask for room nine or ten.

CHAPTER 11

THE HOLLOWAY

C onnecting Barrack Street and
Market Place, The Holloway
was originally forged through the
Warwick rock to ease the gradient
for carts travelling from Saltisford.
The English name Holloway (hol-
low-way) derives from the Old English 'hola weg' meaning a sunken
road. The modern-day Holloway
remains a unique site in the town,
bookended by public houses and
lined with tables and chairs at the
Barrack Street end. When filled with locals and tourists, the
area has a very vibrant, European-style atmosphere.

A terrace of large imposing properties once stood over-
looking The Holloway. One of these grand buildings had
been the home for several generations of local resident John's
family. John now retired and living in one of the modern

properties situated on the site of these old dwellings tells an intriguing story, one regaled in detail through his family for generations.

His great, great grandparents, George, and Hannah (known as Nance) occasionally took in visitors to the town. Boarding houses were common in the 1800s, where those with the extra space, would let out rooms as a source of extra income. Paying guests ranged from racegoers, visitors to the castle and others merely breaking their journeys enroute to other destinations.

While the extra income was of course welcomed, those with less forthcoming character would be treated with suspicion and there would be a sense of relief when they checked out without incident. George and Nance are known to have been very particular, insisting that the strict rules of the house were adhered to by all patrons. There had been some occasions where rowdy racegoers had returned inebriated after a successful day at the races and were promptly asked to vacate their rooms and find accommodation elsewhere.

While the properties sadly no longer stand in their original form, one guest left a mysterious legacy. A gentleman calling himself John Webster had asked if he could rent a room for one or possibly two nights as he had some unexpected spare time to fill on his business trip to the area. The man spoke with a soft Scottish accent and gave the air of an extremely well-educated individual. Very well heeled, dressed in a dark tailored suite typical of the mid-1800s, and sporting a perfectly groomed moustache, the man complimented his appearance with a fine ebony handled Malacca walking cane with a highly polished brass tip.

To all intents and purposes Mr Webster was the ideal guest, but Nance had a very uneasy feeling about the funereal, albeit very dapper man. A very private individual, he gave no specific detail to his profession or business in the area. Webster travelled very lightly carrying only an old leather Gladstone bag upon which the initials JW were embossed in faded gold leaf. He politely requested an early morning call and a light breakfast from his hosts and retired for the night.

The matron of the house is said to have slept uneasily that night, unnerved by the peculiar, insular man sleeping above them in the top room of the house. She awoke very early to prepare her guests light breakfast as requested and Mr Webster appeared on the stroke of seven to take his place at the breakfast table. Less formally attired than the previous evening, his clothes creased from having been crammed into such a small bag, he informed the landlady that he would be dining out in the evening and would probably return around 10pm.

Nance set about completing her chores for the day and, after a late afternoon nap, she began to feel a little unwell, developing quite a headache as she prepared dinner for her husband. She was convinced it was a result of the anxiety she was experiencing around Mr Webster but still couldn't account for why she felt this way.

As dusk approached, she needed to take the air to clear her head and after wrapping up warmly, set off for a long evening stroll. On her route home via St Nicholas's church-yard, she ventured but a few yards when to her astonishment, through the fading light, she saw the figure of a man wandering amongst the tombstones. Drawing closer, she recognised the man. It was John Webster, pen in hand and making notes.

Until the enactment of the Anatomy Act of 1832 in Brit-ain, the taking of corpses from graves was, by technicality, not illegal. Prior to the act, a corpse had no legal standing, and as such, was not owned by anybody. Theft of items other than the corpse was however illegal, so 'body snatchers' as they were often known, would leave everything but the body in the coffin. Those in receipt of corpses were often in medical education and often had little care how bodies had been obtained or who paid for them, ensuring that trade and business remained rife during the 18th and 19th century. Legal or illegal, the practice was both morally and religiously reprehensible to most upstanding members of society. Overcome by what she had witnessed Nance hurried home to tell her husband that she had been right to be suspicious of the man who was obviously up to no good, and he would have to leave immediately. George tried to calm her. He considered that, as the man had already paid for two nights, they were obligated to honour the arrangement. Webster returned precisely at 10pm that evening and went straight to his room. A second sleepless night followed for Nance but by the time she rose early the next day, the mysterious guest had already left.

Preparing the room for the next visitor with some trepidation, the couple were relieved to find no specific evidence of nefarious graveyard activity. Whilst cleaning under the bed, Nance did however find the immaculate Malacca cane that their guest had on their person when arriving at the boarding house. It was initially kept in their custody, should Mr Webster ever reappear to recover the personal and valuable item. As a church going and highly religious lady, Nance became increasingly uncomfortable about keeping the cane in the property, an item she felt carried menace and had touched the hands of a man carrying out the devil's work. Her husband promised to dispose of it but, unbeknown to her, passed it to her son for safe keeping.

Years and generations have passed but the fine, early Victorian cane remains in the family along with the story to go alongside it. John is now the keeper of it and still polishes the hallmarked silver collar bearing an inscription to the mysterious guest 'John Webster'. The story has always intrigued the family, but it wasn't until relatively recently that, by pure chance some information that could have a bearing on the matter came to light. John's cousin, who also lives in Warwick, discovered papers written by a John Webster following his visit to the town in 1857.

Titled 'Grave-Yard Statistics of Warwick and Leamington', and also available to view online, the John Webster of these published papers, was a Scottish Doctor of Medicine. He is known to have travelled widely in Europe, spending three years visiting and studying at some of the most important and scientific institutions of the time. He recounts his visit to Warwickshire and studies of gravestone records and provides a fascinating account and comparison between the towns of Warwick and Leamington during that period.

The rediscovery of spa waters in Leamington Priors in the late 1700s resulted in both a population and popularity explosion, attracting the wealthy and famous, keen to drink and bathe in the supposedly restorative waters. Yet, Webster's investigations imply that those same visitors should have perhaps been visiting neighbouring Warwick if restoration was their goal.

Webster notes how "according to existing memorials in the churchyards of Warwick, from eighty to ninety years appear to be not uncommon ages; several exceeded that period; while one woman buried in the St Nicholas cemetery, had attained ninety-two at death. Contrasted with Warwick, the burial grounds of Leamington indicated much lower ages; no individual buried in any cemetery in Leamington is named as having reached ninety years, as far as I could ascertain; eighty-eight being the highest figure reported on any gravestone." He proffers Warwick's 'favourable' position and 'free ventilation' in several streets as explanation. In comparison the recently renamed Royal Leamington Spa of the time was reported as 'near to the banks of a muddy, sluggish stream, which cannot but be insalubrious', contrary to any public perception.

Webster later worked in lunatic asylums, hospitals, and workhouses on the continent and Great Britain and helped to pioneer many improvements in these institutions. Whether the cane in John's possession belonged to the published John Webster or a body snatcher bearing the same name, remains a point of debate, much like the long-standing debate over which town is the crown of Warwick District. Many Warwick residents won't disagree with Dr John Webster though, who concluded in his paper that there was 'sufficient proofs…to warrant the inference that Warwick is a more salubrious and preferable residence than Leamington.'

CHAPTER 12

WARWICK CASTLE

There has been much written and recorded about the ghosts of Warwick Castle and indeed modern-day owners of the mighty fortress have used these legends to great effect in their commercial enterprises. Ghost hunts and paranormal investigations are frequently carried out and numerous films and documentaries have been recorded at the site.

The Watergate Tower or 'ghost tower', as it has been named, is allegedly haunted by the ghost of Fulke Greville, Lord Brooke. Greville was an Elizabethan poet and dramatist. He also served in the House of Commons as chancellor of the exchequer and commissioner of the treasury – roles which later gained him peerage. He was granted a rather dilapidated Warwick Castle by King James I in 1604 and spent thousands restoring it. His own dramatic finale occurred in 1628 when he was murdered by his most trusted servant Ralph Haywood. Haywood stabbed Greville at his home, believing that his employer was attempting to cheat him in his will. Hayward then turned the knife upon himself. Some may ultimately lay the death of Greville at the hands of the physicians treating him rather than Hayward, as the pig fat they filled the punctures with ended up infecting his wounds. Greville succumbed to his injuries 4 weeks after the initial stabbing.

The body of Greville is laid to rest beneath a magnificent tomb in the church of St Mary in Warwick which carries an epitaph composed by Greville himself:

Folk Grevill
Servant to Queen Elizabeth
Concellor to King James
and Frend to Sir Phillip Sidney
Trophaeum Peccati

The two Latin words, Tropheaum Peccati translate roughly to mean 'Sin's Trophy'. A most pertinent, haunting, and evocative summary of his life. As well as inhabiting the Watergate tower where he spent his final agonising days, Greville's restless spirit has also been sighted wandering the corridors of his former home, ever since his death.

Paranormal activity within the confines of the medieval castle is not just limited to murdered noblemen. It is also said that in the darkest, deepest recesses of the castle, a sinister entity haunts the former dungeon. This malevolent spirit is believed to be that of a sadistic former jailer who took immense pleasure from torturing the prisoners who were entrusted to him. The disfigured face of the jailer has been seen staring out from behind a metal grate screaming at unsuspecting visitors. Some claim to have been assaulted by him, with scratches and bruising testifying to his sinister activities.

The disembodied footsteps of long dead military men have been heard marching around the courtyards of the castle and tales have also been told of the mournful wailing of a distraught woman believed to have been walled up with her infant child over two centuries after the unspeakable act.

⚜

The shadow of a woman believed to be Anne Greville has also been witnessed following visitors throughout the building. The 4th Countess of Warwick, born 1829, was known to be fascinated by ghosts and was convinced that the castle was haunted by many spirits. Her eldest son and heir is recorded as saying, 'like many other very old houses, Warwick Castle is said to be haunted, but for reasons that are doubtless perfectly satisfactory no ghost has ever honoured me with a visit. My mother used to hear strange and uncanny noises; I never succeeded in doing as much as that.'

Anne Greville lived in an era where there was great interest in the spiritual world with seances being a popular pastime amongst many. In the late 1800s she held seances at the castle accompanied by some very eccentric characters. Frances (Daisy) Greville the 5th Countess was also known to have held seances too. Two particularly notorious individuals known to have attended these events were Archdeacon Colley, rector in nearby Stockton between 1901 – 1912, and

Aleister Crowley the English occultist born in neighbouring Leamington Spa.

Colley was a spiritualist, 'high' churchman and was a friend of Sir Arthur Conan Doyle. Although the Archdeacon undertook many good works for his parishioners he was also known for his oft bizarre behaviour. He had a glass topped coffin made for him which he would lie in dressed in his robes and be carried around the church. He claimed this was to demonstrate that he was not afraid of dying. The coffin was kept in his study and those that attended confirmation classes had to sit on it. Colley would claim to have taken many photographs of alleged spirits during prayer meetings at Stockton rectory and believed he foresaw the death of his friend the famous journalist William Stead on the Titanic in 1912. Stead, another spiritualist with interests in psychical research and a self-proclaimed ability to able to contact spirits by telepathy and automatic writing, would no doubt hold pity that neither Colley nor any other spirits seemingly warned him of his fate before he boarded the doomed vessel.

Born in Leamington on October 12th, 1875, Aleister Crowley was once dubbed 'The Wickedest Man in the World' and he referred to himself as the 'Great Beast 666'. He dabbled in occultism, philosophy, poetry, painting, writing, mountaineering and ceremonial 'magick'. Identifying himself as a prophet he founded the so-called religion of Thelema described as a Western esoteric and occult social or spiritual philosophy. The mystical societies he founded some said were merely simply pretexts for him to experiment with as many drugs and to seduce as many women, or men, as he could. Whilst he had his initiates and admirers in his day, including Anne and Frances Greville, his cult status grew after his death in 1947.

Relatively recently two transcripts of seances held at Warwick castle by Anne Greville were discovered in amongst other personal documents hidden away by the late Countess. It appears that her motivation for staging these events was to attempt to encourage the ghosts of the castle to refrain from noisy and disturbing activity in certain rooms of the ancient building. The seances were conducted in what was originally called the Oak Bedroom but later renamed the Kenilworth Bedroom.

The first of these recordings was written in what was described as 'a very loose hand'. Very likely scrawled by the countess herself, it seemed to be consistent with the technique of 'spirit' or 'automatic' writing. It is alleged that both transcripts centre around the ghost of an old servant by the name of Edward Jameson who appears to have been accused of making noises around the castle rooms. The first message begins:

'Leave all to the future research. The Power at work is not that of the mortals in the Castle of here. The Spirit of my called Edward Jameson is one of these who now haunt the place'

The interpretation of this is that this ghost had stolen something from the household in the past and in searching for his hidden bounty was assisted in his noise making by two other spirits.

The second transcript is written in a very different way. This seems to capture an attempt to encourage a conversation with a ghost or spirit using the services of a medium. Questions are asked and they appear to elicit responses from two other ghostly servants called Richard Leigh and Sarah Kitchener. Attempts are made to encourage the spirit of Edward Jameson to give up the 'secret' or location of a stolen item hidden somewhere in the castle's rooms. The Countess, accompanied by her son Lord Brooke and a close friend, possibly Lady Ashburton, seem to have visited several bedrooms in order to find out which room contained his 'secret'. A map was discovered which indicated that it must have been a set of rooms in the upstairs of the western end of the castle.

The papers and Archdeacon Colley's involvement may be indicative of an assumption at the time that any spiritual world would still centre around their Christian faith. Both documents ask the ghost if prayers would be the answer to setting the spirits free. Whether or not Anne's efforts to get the ghosts to cease their noisy activity was successful is unknown, however some spiritual success is recorded on a notice in the Kenilworth Room at the castle today that reads:

'RAISING A GIRL FROM THE DEAD – According to tradition, Anne 4th Countess of Warwick and the renowned South African spiritualist Archdeacon Colley raised a young girl from the dead on a bed in this room'.

At the time Lord Brooke commented that 'He (Colley) brought a medium from Birmingham, and I believe they raised, or saw a little girl carrying flowers. I can only hope they were satisfied'. As far as Aleister Crowley's attendance at any of the seances is concerned, one can only speculate and shudder at what his motives might have been!

A local man reminded me of a curious tale told many years ago about the famous Dun Cow of Warwick. The tale however is not the famous story about the slaying of the mythical beast by the legendary Guy of Warwick, but of a visit to Warwick Castle in the 1880s by Lady Downshire and her husband, Lord Downshire. The Dowager Marchioness of Downshire was in fact related to the Greville family of Warwick.

During her visit, the then Lady Warwick, mentioned casually to her guests that fresh turf had been laid down on a grass plot under the windows of the rooms allotted to the Downshire's for their stay. Her request made that she 'hoped no one would walk on the new turf until it had taken good root', challenged as it was while Warwick was bathed in hot sunshine. It was a glorious summer, however, Lady Downshire was known to suffer in the heat. She always found it oppressive and had great difficulty sleeping. One particularly warm morning during her stay the Dowager got up at dawn to open the window and she saw, to her astonishment, a dun-coloured cow trampling over the newly laid turf. Having regard to Lady Warwick over the freshly laid grass, she tried frantically to shoo away the heavy-footed intruder. By now Lord Downshire had awoken and joined his wife in attempting to frighten the beast away. The creature took not the slightest notice of their joint command to 'keep off the grass' however.

Lord Downshire commented, 'Must have escaped from a herd in the park' before returning to bed to try and return to sleep, cross but also anxious about the reaction of Lady Warwick to the damaged turf. After a further short restless period of attempted sleep herself, Lady Downshire rose and on looking out of the window was astonished. She summoned her husband to view what they had anticipated would be a decimated area of lawn. However, no hoof marks were visible, the turf immaculate, instead sparkled with dew.

At breakfast later that morning the Downshire's sat, bleary eyed, staring at each other across the table unable to make sense of the strange experience they had both encountered. It had not been a dream as they had both seen the creature. But how to explain the fact that the turf had remained untouched was impossible.

There was a legend that always struck fear into the hearts of the family residing at the Castle and which was never spoken about. It was said that the Dun Cow always appeared before a death in the Warwick family. Lady Downshire, knowing nothing of the legend, innocently related her experience to Lady Warwick, her tale backed up by her husband. Neither seemed to observe Lady Warwick's pallor turning grey and the couple continued to talk about the events of the early morning. They could not understand why a sense of gloom suddenly fell upon the breakfast table.

Shortly after the breakfast table had been cleared, Lady Warwick confided to Lady Downshire that she herself had previously seen the spectral cow, concluding tearfully 'and you will hear very shortly that one or another of us has passed away'. Her words proved prophetic. A few weeks later Lord Warwick died.

❧

A lesser told haunting from the Castle has its origins in the early part of the 20th century. The River Island, as it is known on the other side of the river from the Castle, has been used for many purposes over the centuries. Jousting, feasting and many other activities have taken place here. The presence of the famous Peacocks that freely roam the Castle grounds dates to the 1890s. The popular feathered residents were kept as part of a menagerie on the River Island created by the 5th Countess of Warwick. At that time the peacocks were accompanied by an emu, elephant, deer and what was called at the time an ant bear, more commonly known today as an aardvark.

An unexplained phenomenon on the bank of the River Island has been recorded on occasions in the past. Witnesses and observers to the phenomena, report seeing a hazy manifestation of a gentleman in uniform lying on the bank, a stag standing over him staring down at his seemingly lifeless body. The tale of what happened to an unfortunate groom in the service of Lord Warwick may well account for this strange apparition.

A newspaper excerpt from 1903 reads: 'Charles Dove, aged about sixty years, a groom in the employ of Lord Warwick, met with a shocking death on Sunday. About four o'clock in the afternoon he went on to an island in the Avon, which forms part of the castle grounds, and on which are kept a number of Chinese and Japanese deer. At a quarter past six he was found outside the enclosure of wire netting in a dying condition, suffering frightful wounds, to which he succumbed shortly after he was discovered. 'He had been attacked by a Chinese buck, but had managed to clamber over the railings, which are six feet in height. Lord Warwick immediately shot the beast which was itself covered with its victim's blood.'

CHAPTER 13

WITCHES FROM WARWICK

Witchcraft was not made a capital offence in Britain until 1563 although it was deemed heresy and was denounced as such by Pope Innocent VIII in 1484. From 1484 until around the mid-1700s some 200,000 witches were tortured, burnt, or hanged in Western Europe.

Most supposed witches were usually old women and invariably poor. Any who were unfortunate enough to be 'crone like', snaggle toothed, sunken cheeked and having a hairy lip were assumed to possess the 'Evil Eye'. Even in this modern day, it is thought that around 40% of the world's population still believe in the power of the evil eye; the ability to curse another individual through a malevolent glare. Eye beads, often made from glass, are perhaps the most familiar talismans still in prevalent use to help protect from the evil eye. Many readers may have brought eye beads back home as souvenirs from Mediterranean holidays, unaware of their intended purpose or alleged powers.

If an individual also had a cat this too could be condemning, as witches were thought to often have a 'familiar'. Depending on your perspective, familiars are either helpful spirits, or demons, serving and assisting a witch with their powers. They are often said to assume the form of an animal, the cat being the most common. Such suspicions could condemn around 12.5 million cat owners in the UK today.

Many unfortunate women were condemned on this sort of evidence and hanged after undergoing appalling torture. The 'pilnie-winks' (thumb screws) and iron 'caspie-claws' (a form of leg irons heated over a brasier) usually extracted a confession from the supposed witch. Ducking or cucking stools were chairs formerly used for punishment of so called 'disorderly' women. In medieval times until the early 18th century, ducking was a way used to establish whether a suspect was a witch. The ducking stools were first used for this purpose, but ducking was later inflicted without the chair. In this case the subject's right thumb was bound to her left big toe. A rope was tied around the waist of the accused, and she was thrown into a river or deep pond. If she floated, it was deemed that, in rejecting the baptismal water, she was in league with the devil as destined for execution. If she sank, she was 'cleared' and drowned. A no win situation for any accused.

Witch fever gripped East Anglia for 14 terrible months between 1645 – 1646. The people of these eastern counties were solidly Puritan and rabid anti-Catholics and easily swayed by bigoted preachers whose mission was to seek out the slightest whiff of heresy. A man called Matthew Hopkins, an unsuccessful lawyer, came to prominence. He became known as the 'Witchfinder General'. After Chelmsford he set off for Norfolk and Suffolk. Aldeburgh paid him £6 for clearing the town of witches, Kings Lynn £15 and a grateful Stowmarket £23. This was at a time when the daily wage was 2.5p. Many of Matthew Hopkins theories of deduction were based on Devil's Marks. A wart or mole or even a flea bite he took to be a Devil's Mark and he used his 'jabbing needle' to see if these marks were insensitive to pain. His 'needle' was a 3-inch-long spike which retracted into the spring-loaded handle, so the unfortunate woman never felt any pain.

A last reminder of Hopkin's reign of terror was discovered in St. Osyth, Essex in 1921. Two female skeletons were found in a garden, pinned into unmarked graves and with iron rivets driven through their joints. This was to make sure a witch could not return from the grave. Hopkins was responsible for over 300 executions. He had 68 people put to death in Bury St Edmunds alone, and 19 hanged at Chelmsford in a single day.

In the year 1646, during the height of the East Anglia witch hunts, namesake Ellen Garrison was accused of witchcraft in the village of Upswell. Like her mother before her, Ellen was said by those who knew the family to be a witch. Accused of murdering children and entertaining evil spirits, the case against her looked bleak; but perhaps Witchfinder General Matthew Hopkins had met his match.

On the 1st August 1646 Ellen, wife of thatcher Robert Garrison, was accused of bewitching two of local butcher Robert Parson's children, who subsequently died, and for entertaining evil spirits. Locals told tales of losing animals due to curses from Ellen, others claimed that beetles and crickets had warned them of impending visits from the witches' imps and demons. A local midwife claimed Ellen's 'teats' were of an 'extraordinary nature' thus proving she was possessed.

Furthermore, the local constable along with four other men had visited the Garrison household with the intention of pressing one of Ellen's sons for the army. Unsurprisingly it was said Ellen reacted very badly and flew into a witch's frenzy, cursing the five men. The men claimed that several weeks later they had all lost animals as a direct result of the curse.

Ellen was imprisoned on 22nd September 1646 and sent for trial two days later with two other women accused of witchcraft. Matthew Hopkins himself attended the trial. It had all the hallmarks of leading to hangings, but miraculously all three women were acquitted. The murder charge against Ellen was thrown out on a technicality and all the other accusations were not proven. A disastrous result for Hopkins and possibly the beginning of the end for the witch hunter.

❧

As fear of witches spread throughout the country, whispers, and gossip in Warwick amongst the 'common people' led women and young girls to the gallows for crimes allegedly associated with witchcraft. Often these were very sad and distressing cases. The murder of infants by allegedly possessed women were in many cases the result of unwanted pregnancies, the shame of which was unbearable for unmarried women. Mental health conditions and epilepsy were often construed as devil or demon possession for which women were tortured and executed. Scolding or backbiting was also associated with witchcraft.

John Crump from Warwick was a physician and astrologer. In the 1640s his daughter Hannah was recorded to be 'afflicted by witchcraft' for nearly two years. It was said that little Hannah was deeply disturbed and suffered 'strange fits'. Her father, fearful that she might possibly be thought of as a witch, decided to take Hannah to London where it was said there were people who could 'cure' witches. Upon arriving in the capital, Hannah succumbed to one of her strange fitting episodes and was taken immediately to St Thomas Hospital in Southwark. Her manner it was said was such that the medics refused to attend to her saying she was 'fitter for Bedlam than to come into a hospital among sick people'. Interestingly the term bedlam comes the name of a hospital in London, 'Saint Mary of Bethlehem' which was devoted to treating the mentally ill in the 1400s. Over time, the pronunciation of 'Bethlehem' morphed into 'bedlam' and the term came to be applied to any situation where pandemonium prevails.

Following the hospitals refusal to treat Hannah her father sought out the services of what was known as a 'cunning man' (a person also known as a folk healer or wise person who was a practitioner of 'magic' in Britain from the Middle Ages to as late as the early 20th century). This man who also claimed to be a physician lived in Winchester Park in Southwark.

'Cunning folk' were generally sly imposing characters who adapted to changing circumstances and were good at spotting new opportunities. We would perhaps consider them 'con men' nowadays. Their fees depended on what they thought their clients could afford but they were seldom cheap and sometimes astronomical. People were divided in their opinions of cunning folk. In some communities they were very well respected and even asked to be godparents to local children. Critics however regarded them as persons of 'ill fame and of dishonest persuasion', charlatans and imposters who prospered from deceit and unwilling to make their livelihood by honest means.

After considering Hannah's medical history the cunning-man confirmed she was bewitched and offered to cure her for five pounds. However, to do this he said he would have to take on the bewitchment himself. Someone he claimed had to bear the curse once it was made and if it wasn't the witch herself or him, one of her familiars could infect someone else with it. Back in Warwick and on hearing of the cunning-man's proposal Hannah's sister suggested that before proceeding they should first try prayer and fasting to see if it might help Hannah with her dispossession. Her family subsequently gathered and proceeded to pray. However, during prayers, it is said that Hannah leapt from her bed 'in a very great race' tearing at her clothes and crying out in a lamentable manner.

Although there were periods when Hannah quietened down, she still resisted assistance, kicking her father, and continuing to try to burn herself and her family members, breaking windows, and bizarrely demanding a pipe to smoke tobacco. She claimed during prayers that her illness befell her after she consumed an apple a woman brought her in her sickness. Her family turned their prayers towards stopping the witch's powers, but Hannah resisted violently, spitting at her father.

Despite the dreadfully distressing events, the dedicated Warwick family continued to pray until the late evening when suddenly Hannah became peaceful and serene in her bed as if a great weight had suddenly been lifted from her. Upon waking Hannah asked for a bible and read it for several hours after which she appeared totally normal. John Crump, his family, and his daughter Hannah rejoiced as she appeared to be dispossessed of her affliction which never affected her again. Some weeks later when they were convinced of her recovery the Crump family attended St Mary's church in Warwick to give thanks for Hannah's seeming deliverance from witchcraft.

Like the case of Ellen Garrison, it was unusual for a girl or woman, accused of the serious charges of witchcraft during that era, to escape an unhappy ending. Curiously it is said that the ghostly figure of a young woman has been seen at the side of the tumbrel in the crypt of St Mary's. Dressed in a smock and bonnet she smiles contentedly ... could this conceivably be the ghost of Hannah demonstrating how she was spared the fate of many unfortunate women of her time.

❦

Possibly the most well-known of the folklore tales of alleged Witches associated with Warwick is that of Moll Bloxam. It is said that Moll was an old milk maid employed at Warwick Castle in the 1700s. She dedicated her working life to the Earl of Warwick and was loyal to him until her retirement. As an acknowledgement of her long service the Earl granted Moll permission to sell any surplus milk and butter from the castle to the good people of the town.

Local women quickly realised however, that Moll was deceiving them by charging for pints of milk whilst not giving them a full measure. They ensured that news of this duplicity reached the ears of the Earl, who was left angry that Moll had abused his kind gesture.

The fate of Moll Bloxham is subject to conjecture. Some tales record that she was ordered to be cast out of the town and never allowed to return. Others have it that she was subject to egregious torture at the hands of the Earl, before succumbing to her injuries. However Moll departed the town, all accounts agree that her final act was one of Witchcraft, placing a curse on both the town and the Earl himself, swearing that Warwick would never be free of her.

Not long after Moll had departed, guards from the castle witnessed an incredible phenomenon in Mill Street, the street in which Moll Bloxham had plied her cheating trade. They saw a huge black dog with flaming red eyes menacingly walking towards them. Before they could take evasive action, the dog leapt onto the ramparts of the castles and disappeared. Legend has it that, during the following weeks, every housewife who had complained about Moll was discovered mauled to death in the alleyways of the town. With speculation rife that Moll Bloxham had returned in diabolical form, the Black Dog was pursued through the streets of the town and into the castle. Cornered high up in Caesar's tower, a servant is said to have tricked the beast into leaping from the tower to its demise as it became trapped in the weir below.

Even now, many believe that the town of Warwick is still not free of Moll Bloxham, just as she had warned. It is said that from time-to-time Moll, in the shape of a black dog, can be seen on the castle ramparts and in the streets around the castle. A sighting as recent as 2020 has been claimed. The vision of a grey lady in and around Warwick Castle has also been attributed to the spirit of this most vengeful witch.

"

Tis now the very witching time of night,
When churchyards yawn, and hell itself breathes out
Contagion to this world: now could I drink hot blood
And do such bitter business as the day
Would quake to look on.

William Shakespeare

CHAPTER 14

THE MILL GARDEN

At the end of Mill Street, overlooked by Caesar's tower from where the black dog tumbled to its demise, is the magnificent Mill Garden. With Warwick Castle as a stunning and dramatic backdrop, the Mill Garden was landscaped over a period of 60 years by Arthur Measures; a gentleman with an exceptionally interesting history whose kindness is legend in the town. Born in Manchester in 1909, at aged one, Arthur was brought by his parents to Warwick. They were master and matron of the workhouse and brought up their family of six in squalid conditions that still prevailed in such environments, even after the end of the Victorian era. Such a start in life did not prevent Arthur from achieving success and he became the manager of the main Birmingham branch of Barclays bank, a role which ultimately secured the future of Mill Street for the town.

Arthur married Violet Bray, a local Warwick girl, in 1936 and together, they moved into the cottage at the end of Mill Street and began planting his beautiful garden. In 1959 the residents of Mill Street learned that the cottages were to be put up for sale at auction by the Earl of Warwick, as a job lot for development, an approach that excluded residents from bidding to secure their own properties. With a Birmingham property developer keen and lurking, Arthur Measures, using a Barclays loan of course, organised a syndicate and outbid all other interested parties, buying all the cottages for £610,000, guaranteeing the immediate future of his friends and neighbours and securing the unique idyl that everyone can enjoy today. Arthur originally opened his gardens for visitors for a single weekend to raise funds to restore St Mary's Church tower. The unquenchable benevolence of Arthur & Violet continued unabated as they further acquired a string of charities, ultimately opening their gardens to paying visitors between Easter and October in support of them all. Arthur sadly died at the grand age of 90 in 1999. The unmissable garden, however, remains open to this day to visitors in his memory and in the support of charities.

Dating from around 1650, a set of old wooden stocks are situated just inside the Mill Garden, reminding us of a time when torture and punishment were commonplace. The infliction of pain and torture were accepted means of punishment or interrogation for centuries across Great Britain. The method of punishment inflicted often varied depending on the crime or social status of the victim. Cruel and sadistic torturers are said to have taken visible pleasure in inflicting horror on the accused, and stocks were one device frequently used throughout the 16th & 17th century, their use not declining until into the 18th century.

The stocks were a wooden structure formerly in use both on the continent of Europe and in Great Britain as a method of punishment for petty offences, with whipping posts, pillories or even gallows reserved for more serious crimes. Those condemned to the stocks, sat on a wooden bench with ankles and sometimes wrists or even neck, thrust through holes in moveable boards.

It is thought that the word 'stock' first appeared in English in 862, being adapted from Germanic language where it was used in reference to a 'tree trunk' or 'stump'. Exactly how the word became associated with corporal punishment has been lost to history. It seems the use of the word and meaning was widely prevalent and understood by 1530; somewhat ironic given how its etymology now remains contested nearly 500 years later. It is thought by some that the term 'laughing stock' originated from the use of stock. An easy link to make given how those in stocks would have no doubt been humiliated as they were put on display to the crowd for their crimes. At one time someone who was accused of something was known as a 'pointing stock' and someone frequently beaten with a whip was known as a 'whipping stock'. There are linguists who argue however, that there is no definitive evidence connecting these familiar turns of phrase with the once regular form of justice.

Punishment in the stocks generally lasted for several hours at least. During this time passers-by would throw all forms of foul, decomposing detritus at the hapless victim. Some places specified only 'soft material' could be thrown, effectively preventing victims from being stoned (or potatoed) to death. If the person was popular or well liked, they might have been showered with flowers or just have their shoes removed and their feet tickled. Every town or village was required by law to have a set of stocks. Perhaps the most frequently used stocks in Warwick were those situated at the Market Hall in the centre of the town. These were replaced in the early 19th century by stocks on wheels which were used until 1872 for drunkenness. Those found guilty of the crime were made to draw the wheeled device to a railed area where the public were at liberty to pelt the victim.

In this most peaceful place, the appearance of the stocks would perceivably be jarring were they not so easily wed with the medieval background. Unsurprisingly, numerous tales associated with this relic of history have been recounted over the years.

Several years ago, a couple staying in the town during the cold winter months, decided to venture to Mill Street on an evening walk. The unique setting, cobbled streets and sight of Warwick Castle make for a popular photo opportunity at any time of the year; however, the dark can assist in producing fabulously evocative, romantic and, perhaps even haunting, images at the site. There is no through passage at the end of Mill Street, as large gates block an entrance to the castle grounds and an adjacent hedge shields the Mill Garden from the street. Whilst taking snaps, the couple recount how they were drawn to a glow behind the hedgerow. Peering curiously through gaps in the foliage, both claim to have witnessed a foggy 'blue-grey' mist, its presence isolated exclusively around the stocks, before fading and then vanishing suddenly. Although possibly attributable to some kind of atmospheric anomaly, the couple themselves referred to what they saw as "some sort of manifestation".

Another mystery centring around the stocks was told by an American tourist. The man claimed to have photographed a disheveled man locked in the stocks; a spectacle which he at the time assumed was staged for the interest and amusement of holidaying visitors. Later that evening upon looking back at the photographs he had taken that day, only the stocks themselves had been captured on film. He expressed his own anxieties about sharing this experience with friends, family and others, concerned that he himself might end up a 'laughing stock'.

"

'Pray you let us not be laughing stocks to other men's humours: I desire you in friendship, and I will one way or other make you amends.'

William Shakespeare

CHAPTER 15

WEST GATE

M edieval Warwick was once a walled town, and the gates at the end of High Street & Jury Street still stand. The first record of the West Gate entrance to Warwick is as far back as 1126, the Chapel of St James situated above it, paid for by the then Earl of Warwick, Roger de Newburgh. Both gate and chapel were reconstructed again in the late 14th Century by a different Earl of Warwick, Thomas Beauchamp. A tower was erected and a ribbed-barrel vault supporting the passageway was also added during this reconstruction, producing what is its current shape and appearance. Beauchamp gave jurisdiction for the Chapel of St James to the newly created Guild of St George the Martyr, who duly extended it to include a Great Hall and accommodation.

On the north side there are traces of an earlier wall and vault which were possibly part of a narrower passage. The parapet walk along the top of the town wall had originally skirted the east end of the chapel. After the town wall was breached and the roadway diverted to the south of the gate, the walks along the south and east sides of the chapel appear to have fallen into disuse. In 1571, the Earl of Leicester Robert Dudley, acquired all the buildings and repurposed them as a hospital for former soldiers, known at the time as 'The Leycester Hospital'.

The chapel itself was restored and redesigned between 1863 to 1865 by Sir Gilbert Scott, an architect famous for many great achievements not least the design of the iconic red phone box. The east window of the Chapel was bricked up during the religious upheaval of the Tudor period but was opened again when Gilbert Scott restored the decaying medieval building. Even so, the Chapel is still lit solely by candlelight creating a very atmospheric, and some may say, eerie space. In front of the alter is a candleholder hanging from a medieval sculpture in the form of a crown. The east and south windows hold glass by the famous Clayton and Bell company of London. The window over the south door is glazed with a depiction of The Annunciation, designed by English poet, artist, and designer William Morris. On the wall hangs a tapestry, also by Morris. In the chancel are high backed chairs made of bog oak from Ireland, given by a former master of the Lord Leycester Hospital. The alter frontal was made for King George V1's coronation at Westminster Abbey in 1937. It was initially used at the Chapel Royal in the Tower of London before being brought to Warwick.

When the 'Hospital for warriors' was first opened by the Earl of Leicester, there were originally twelve Brethren. In the 1960s the building was renovated, and new larger apartments were created reducing the number of Brethren to eight. Local folklore records that during renovation work at the West gate several relics were discovered beneath the floor of the chapel including old clay pipes and bones. The bones were most probably those of animals discarded after feasts. There is also a story that during the partial reconstruction of a wall in the chapel, the body of a headless knight clad in medieval armour was discovered. For many years prior to this find it was said that a phantom of a headless knight was often seen restlessly skirting the perimeter of the old Hospital. Once the remains of the knight discovered in the wall had been removed and afforded a Christian burial in a local churchyard the hauntings ceased.

Life at the Lord Leycester is like that at the Royal Hospital Chelsea which houses the famous Chelsea pensioners. Although on a smaller scale, the Brethren at Warwick are always proud to tell you that their history is over a century older than their London counterparts. Over the years those who have resided in the rooms, have left an incredible collection of memorabilia to the hospital. These include a sword and breastplate from the battle of Waterloo, pikes from the English civil war, a sword from the Crimea and a whole host of war medals.

The Master and Brethren of the Lord Leycester Hospital gather for prayers in the chapel, every weekday at 9.30am and the service is a specially shortened version established by Dudley. Robert Dudley, was very specific in who could become a 'Brother', and this was laid out in the Rules and Ordinances book when the hospital was opened. It was made clear that homes at the hospital would only be provided for Elizabethan soldiers who had been wounded in war. The current day Brethren, attired in their ceremonial Elizabethan dress, are always delighted to accompany visitors around the building and will regale you with some fascinating ancient stories as well the history of the place.

One of the veterans, Bill, has a particularly fascinating story which, although not directly related to Warwick, is worth telling.

During the years immediately following World War II, Bill served in the Royal Navy as leading stoker aboard HMS Vigo. A stoker was a sailor who specialised in engine room duties, spending most of his time in the steering gear room overseeing, amongst other things, the maintenance of the evaporator or distilling apparatus. This was particularly important for all on board, as functioning apparatus produced fresh drinking water from sea water by distillation. Vigo was a battle class destroyer launched in 1945 and named after the battle of Vigo which took place in 1702.

Banter and tall stories have always been part of the camaraderie of the British forces with the Navy having its own peculiar superstitions and rituals. For example, it was believed that it was unlucky to wear the clothes of a sailor who had died at sea. It was also said that by throwing an old broom overboard in the direction desired, a wind could be summoned. Gun salutes are always odd numbers because it's considered bad luck to let it be known how many guns a ship carries. One superstition adopted by the Crew of HMS Vigo was to make a little cotton mannequin out of surplus cleaning cloths. Those aboard the vessel believed that, worn on the lapels of their overalls, these effigies would prevent the wearer from coming to any harm whilst at sea.

A steel grate panel covered the access to the collection of switches, dials, pipes, and hydraulics in the HMS Vigo gear room and once removed, sailors had to descend several very narrow steel ladders into the bowels of the ship. Bill normally took what was known as the 'middle watch' between 12 midnight and 4am and spent those hours alone. One night whilst on watch, the experienced sailor suddenly realised there was a major problem. A valve fixed high above him in the gear room had jammed suddenly, and if the issue wasn't resolved immediately, the consequent buildup of pressure would lead to a catastrophe. In a frantic state, he raced up the narrow ladders as quickly as he could, but on reaching the faulty valve, found to his astonishment that somehow, it had been miraculously turned off, averting what would have almost certainly been a terrible disaster. Looking up through the grating Bill's heart skipped several beats. Staring down at him was a giant of a man. Bearded and smiling, he wore the uniform of an 18th century seaman, a cotton mannequin tucked in his lapel. As soon as Bill opened his mouth to acknowledge him, he was gone.

❧

Hidden behind the ancient buildings of the Lord Leycester Hospital is the enchanting and peaceful Master's Garden, an important part of this unique establishment. This historic plot, enclosed by the town wall of Warwick, has been cultivated for over 500 years. It was restored in both the 1800s and the 1990s. On his acquisition, Robert Dudley decreed that the lower half of the garden be left "green-sward (an expanse of short grass) for recreation". In 1852 the lower half was restored to its original condition and use. Here the brethren played bowls and billiards (but were strictly forbidden to play cards!).

Enclosed by the ancient stone town walls, the garden contains some interesting features. The 12th Century Norman arch between the magnolias was discovered under the Chapel of St James during the restoration of the Chapel in 1860 and was re-erected in its present location. The huge stone vase is reputed to be a 2000-year-old "Nilometer" which crowned one of the columns that stood on the banks of the Nile, used for measuring the height of the river's floods. This was the basis for levels of annual taxation on agricultural land. Renowned luminaries Nathaniel Hawthorne, Charles Dickens, Charles Darwin, and Oscar Wilde are all known to have visited this wonderful and inspiring nirvana.

Sandra, a local lady, worked as a gardener at the hospital for nearly three decades and grew to know every nook and cranny of the ancient building. She still fondly recalls her days there and misses it very much. She was privileged to have her own set of keys so was regularly in the building long after visitors had left and often encountered a shadowy figure, of what she took to be a monk, stooped with hands clasped out in front, just inside the entrance of the Great Hall. The head of the apparition was covered by a cowl, and it wore a long robe. On the first couple of occasions, she admits understandably that she was petrified, but over time she became able to anticipate its appearance by a sudden drop in the room temperature, after which she would attempt to reassure the figure saying, "it's only me". This reassurance seemed to encourage the figure to linger a little longer enabling her to see it more clearly. Sandra claims that the visitations continued for several years until suddenly it ceased to appear.

Her experiences were not confined solely to the Great Hall though. Alarms would be mysteriously activated during the night with no explanation. In the Guildhall flat, Sandra would often hear what she described as medieval music, like an Elizabethan madrigal. A member of the brethren in the

Chapel flat would regularly summon her, complaining of a heavy banging on his door. On each occasion when the door was opened there was no one there and an immediate search of the adjoining parapet area revealed nothing. Another unexplained apparition witnessed by Sandra was that of a man clad in Elizabethan attire gliding across the courtyard balcony and descending the stairs, only never to reappear at the bottom of them. Perhaps the phantom of a previous master.

Members of the public have also had unexplained encounters. One visiting Italian woman and her teenage daughter rushed frantically down the stone steps, from St James chapel in a distressed state one afternoon. A member of the brethren was quickly summoned, as they claimed a dark figure of a man in a long cloak had suddenly appeared in the previously unoccupied room. On investigation of the chapel, there was no sign of any presence.

CHAPTER 16

THE OLD FOURPENNY SHOP

The Old Fourpenny Shop is a Georgian pub, dating from around 1800 and situated at 27/29 Crompton Street. It is a short distance from Warwick town centre and close to the racecourse and castle.

The building sits on the south side of the street on land which, along with adjoining Friars Street and Monks Way, was once the site of a Dominican Friary. The Dominicans, or Black Friars as they were also known, had orders spread throughout Medieval Britain and would actively engage with the local townsfolk rather than isolating themselves behind the closed doors of the Friary. Such an approach meant that,

in comparison to similar religious institutions, the Dominicans were often very popular, and people would gather to listen to their public preachings. The site in Warwick would have been amongst one of the largest of its type in England at the time, with archeologists believing that it would have housed up to 40 monks.

Unfortunately, aside from pertinent street names, there is no physical evidence of the Friary left among the terraced properties and flats that fill the streets today. It was purchased by John, Duke of Northumberland in 1551 and demolished in its entirety after the Dissolution. Stained glass, thought to be from the friary and found in 1835, is now housed at the Warwick Museum.

The Old Fourpenny Shop name derives from the price of a cup of tea and a tot of rum that would be charged to navvies building the nearby Grand Union canal during the early nineteenth century. The old hostelry was formerly known as The Silver Groat named after the ancient English coin worth four pennies. The single split level ground floor room of the pub has a contemporary, relaxed atmosphere and has been a local favourite for many years. Its excellent reputation also attracts visitors and tourists from further afield, the pub also enviably being one of Warwick's few town centre hostelries to benefit from a large garden space. Given the history of the area, it is unsurprising that the pub has its own skeletons in its closet.

Historically, animal bones and human remains have previously been discovered in cellars in the area and archaeological excavations have unearthed several burials which were thought to have been from the friary cemetery. This may well account for occasional unexplained sightings of a monk-like figure who appears to descend the steps at the rear of The Old Fourpenny Shop, only to disappear through the arched aperture below. This would have been an access to the cellar area at one time and the area is said to always remains dank and unpleasantly humid with a strange musty odour.

The most prolific haunting at The Old Fourpenny shop is not a monk however, but the manifestation of a young female phantom. Thought to be a pre-teen, around 12 years of age, her presence in the building has been well documented over many years. She has always been known by the name Winnie. Those who have seen her, describe her as thin, her face framed by hair cut to shoulder length and styled with a straight parting. She is said to wear a very simple, plain dress. Such a description would have been typical of poor children in early to mid-19th century and is consistent of what would be expected in this area of Warwick. Around the mid-19th century, thousands of refugees from the Irish famine would have flooded the lodging houses present in what would have been one of the poorest parts of the town at the time.

Her exact connection with the pub is unknown however, some members of staff claim the girl has spoken to them saying simply, 'I live here, do you?'. The source of her name is also a mystery. If the girl is of Irish origin, as would historically be likely, it is very unlikely that she would have had the name 'Winnie', which is a name of Welsh origin. The Irish equivalent of the name is 'Fionnait', so it may be that, at some point she has been renamed Winnie, simply as it is a name of greater familiarity and ease to those of an English tongue.

Her unexpected appearances in the pub seem to rarely, if ever, cause alarm, and likewise the little girl herself does not appear to be alarmed or perturbed by those she encounters or engages with. Curiously, according to one employee, Winnie appears to have an aversion to anybody who isn't British though. This story in at least in part corroborated by a charming Romanian lady working at the pub, who says she too has encountered the spirit of the girl. Winnie appears to show a dislike to her, always turning away, in seeming disapproval according to the lady, rather than fear of her or discomfort.

Maybe there is nothing more to this than the natural reaction of a little girl faced with an individual of a nationality that she would have never encountered in her short life. Sadly, because of poor sanitary conditions, diseases such as cholera and smallpox would have claimed many a young life in this part of Warwick at time when Winnie would have lived here, and she would likely have been one such victim. That the staff at the pub speak of her presence with fondness and treat her spirit with such respect, offers something of a happy ending to what may otherwise be a somewhat troubling and tragic story.

CHAPTER 17

WEST STREET REVISITED

Leading on from Jury Street, West Street appears to be similarly, one of Warwick's most haunted streets. During the English Civil War, a Tudor property in West Street was used as a look-out post for soldiers. In the modern era the same property was, for a period, a bed and breakfast establishment, its proximity to Warwick Castle being the perfect location for visiting tourists. The owner of the guest house witnessed the apparition of a civil war soldier on numerous occasions as had several guests. Mysterious, heavy footsteps were often heard by the owner when no one else was in the property and guests too, had been unnerved during the night hearing footsteps on the ancient wooden stairs. Curious incidents would occur where electrical devices turned on and off on their own. Battery powered alarm clocks in the upper rooms would also often be found randomly reset and flashing. Cleaners also reported strange happenings including indentations suddenly appearing on the covers of freshly made-up beds.

Contrary to the popular image of the 'cavaliers' versus 'roundheads', attire during the English Civil war varied significantly and, in some instances those on the battlefields would have had trouble distinguishing friend and foe. With the advent of Oliver Cromwell's New Model Army, the whole army was equipped with a coat of a single colour for the very first time. The soldier apparition is described as short in stature with some suggesting he stands barely five feet tall. Wearing a 'lobster pot' helmet, the red coat he adorns is in keeping with that of a parliamentarian soldier of the Cromwellian civil war era. While the presence of a spirit was said to feel the strongest in the upper section of the property, the soldier himself has been witnessed in various rooms throughout the property.

Around the turn of the millennium, the property was subject to scrutiny and investigation by a team of paranormal investigators researching candidate sites for a new television series. The bed and breakfast, by this time was a beautifully decorated and homely Tudor themed hostelry. The ambience throughout was warm and welcoming by day and, with no evidence of the supernatural occurring, the homeowner permitted the team the opportunity to conduct further investigations overnight.

The team positioned themselves and their equipment throughout the property. The antique furnishings in the bedroom named 'The Dressmaker Room', gave the room a slightly gothic chill after sunset. Period paintings added to the quirky ambience of the chamber, and it would be easy to mistake the three antique children's dresses that also hung on the walls for spirits dancing in the darkness. Adding to the unease, sat atop a dressing table was a collection of staring china dolls, very much like those that used to occupy the old dolls museum in Warwick, and which had unnerved many a visitor. Aside from a perhaps understandable feeling of unease in the room, nothing of significant note was recorded in the room. Creaks and knockings were judged to be typical of a building of this type and age, as it cooled at night.

Equipped with an electro-magnetic field (EMF) reader, another member of the investigating team settled in another bedroom, which was known at the time as 'The Kingmaker Room'. EMF readers are widely available and relatively cheap to acquire. It has been theorised that, in the conscious mind, there is an electromagnetic field present that, even when people pass on, doesn't disappear. EMF readers are therefore used in paranormal investigation to try and detect such fluctuations in electric and magnetic energy, to determine the presence of something that was once very human. An odd atmosphere was recorded as persisting in this room along with a humming noise and a faint crackling sound. With no exceptional or anomalous spikes on the EMF reader though it was concluded that these occurrences were most likely down to the unusual number of electrical devices in the room rather than some astral or spiritual activity.

Activity was however experienced by a group of investigators situated in a third, large but comparatively understated bedroom. The team noted the presence of a regular dripping sound but found no evidence of plumbing issues with the sink or toilet in the small ensuite. There were no obvious issues identified in adjoining rooms either. Curiously the dripping was isolated to this bedroom only and, when discussed with the property owner the following morning, there was no known problems with pipework or external guttering. The team were generously afforded the opportunity to investigate this room further the following night.

The team set-up cameras within the room and, to further experimentation, also placed 'trigger' objects around the room in full view of the arranged recording equipment. The use of trigger objects aligns with, what is known throughout ghost hunting circles as, 'The Singapore Theory' or 'Familiarisation Theory'. This theory hypothesises that spirits would be more likely to respond in an environment where sounds or objects that they would have been familiar with are present. In this instance a child's toy was left on the bed, a crucifix left on a bedside table and, a collection of coins and rings left on a large table in the room. When reviewing the footage in the morning, no obvious activity was recorded however, scrolling through the recording at high speed, the team noted that the large table perceptibly moved over the course of the night. A shift of not more than 1 cm was recorded and while this may objectively seem unspectacular, the investigating team needed the strength of three members to move the table any distance themselves. Heavy objects are not ordinarily known to move on their own.

Ultimately, despite these observations, the site was not selected for any further investigations, with the team and producers determining that more actively haunted sites would make better television. Perhaps more time was needed for the spirits to accept the intruders to their world and before revealing themselves further. The property has since been converted into a large and spectacular dwelling house and the current occupants have also had no experiences of the alleged hauntings in the seven years that they have resided there. Maybe the spirits have finally moved on or, possibly, in the fullness of time, the owners will bear witness to para-normal activity themselves.

England is a nation of dog lovers and the sight of an elderly gentleman walking his dog is an everyday occurrence. Owners get into daily walking routines, with many enjoying the solitude of just being with their dog. Others form collective social groups. Whatever the weather the British dog walker is part of daily life. We all know someone who we can set our watch to by their dog walking habits.

Jack Taylor was a well-known figure in Warwick and ran a transport cafe at 62 West Street. Originally from the north-east Jack was a robust character involved with many sporting activities in the Town. 'Old Jacks' as it was known, was a popular stop off point for lorry drivers travelling the length and breadth of the country in the days before the Warwick bypass, when almost all transport had to come through the centre of the town. A classic 'greasy spoon' emporium the business thrived for many years with hungry lorry drivers loving the basic but hearty fare on offer. Jack had served in the Merchant Navy during the second world war and even after losing his wife and closing his business, remained far from lonely. He moved to a house close by and remained very active, regularly frequenting his local pubs on West Street with friends and always accompanied by his little brown and white mongrel dog Tia.

Such was Jack's popularity that the town was in complete shock following events that took place on a dark November night back in 1974. In retirement Jack became an enthusiastic keeper of canaries and was due to attend a prestigious bird show in Oxford on 15th November 1974.

It was odd therefore that, when his son tried to contact him regarding arrangements to attend the show, there was no response. This was so out of character that Jack's son, feeling very concerned, decide to drive from his home in Oxfordshire to Warwick late at night to check on this father's wellbeing. The absolute horror that his son and partner discovered on arrival at Jack's home almost defies description.

Upon entering the house Jack was discovered dead in a huge pool of his own blood, his head battered so severely that he was hardly recognisable. His little dog Tia lay dead beside him, her face and muzzle covered in blood. Blood covered the walls of the hallway with blood-soaked tools scattered everywhere. The house had been ransacked and the horrific scene appeared to be the result of an attempted robbery that had gone horrifically wrong. The perpetrators had however left clues everywhere and within a matter of hours, two men from Birmingham had been traced and apprehended. Jack had been stabbed to death with an old kitchen knife but not before he had been battered by more than twenty hammer blows to his head and shoulders. It had been a frenzied attack by more than one assailant. Despite his age and a heart condition, Jack had obviously put up a spirited fight, as there were bruises and cuts on his arms, described by the pathologist as 'defence wounds' sustained in his heroic attempts to withstand the cowardly onslaught. In trying to defend her master, little Tia had also been brutally stabbed to death. The murderers stood trial in Birmingham in April 1975, and both were sentenced to life imprisonment.

During the mid-1970s up until around 1990 a strange happening occurred on many occasions between the pub previously known as The Vine Inn on West Street and the pub that used to be The Wheatsheaf, which sits at the junction of Crompton Street and West Street. At around ten o'clock in the evening, locals from both establishments reported seeing an elderly man walking his small dog past the pubs. The gentleman on occasions would appear agitated, and was always dressed in an apron, stained heavily with grease and tomato ketchup (or possibly something more sinister). Each time concerned drinkers saw the man and left the premises to enquire as to his wellbeing, he was no longer there.

A similar manifestation was reported as being seen in Crompton Street on the footpath between The Foresters Arms and the junction with Stratford Road. In one instance a women claimed a man answering the same description walking his dog had paused briefly, saying 'hello pet' to her. This was notable as, had he been a local man, he would have been far more likely to address her as 'my duck', a greeting of endearment far more common in the Coventry and War-wickshire area. Before she could return in kind, the man and his dog faded away. The lady was greatly disturbed by the incident, telling her husband on her return home that she had just seen a ghost.

Understandably, there is conjecture that these peculiar historic manifestations in West Street were linked in some way to the terrible events that occurred in this area in 1974. Amidst the horror, there is some reassurance to be found in the thought that for a time, even in the afterlife, Old Jack was able to find solace in his regular walks around the Warwick streets with his beloved Tia.

Another fascinating little tale from West Street is told by a local lady. As a child Joan lived with her parents in a property at the top of the street near to the junction with Bowling Green Street and close to the old Westgate. Her ancestors had always lived in and around the West Street area and a much-treasured family heirloom was the family bible. The great bible of 1539 was the first authorised edition

of the Bible in English, authorised by King Henry VIII of
England 'to be read aloud in the
church services of the Church
of England'. Historically the
family bible was passed down
through the matriarchal side of
the family, given as a gift to the
eldest daughter. It wasn't just a way of passing down a tradition of faith, it was also a family record of births, baptisms,
and deaths. Traditionally many people valued a family tree
bound up together with a godly heritage. The family bible
was considered a wonderful way to treasure family and pass
on stories and family faith from one generation to another.

The early family bibles were usually very large format,
often beautifully bound in leather with large print and beautiful type face. Illustrated in many cases with vibrant colour
plates, which in themselves were works of art, these weighty
volumes occupied pride of place in many a Christian family's
homes. So precious were these books that many believed that
anyone who stole them would be cursed, with many books
having traditional, well-known curses scrawled across their
inside covers in emphasis of this.

Although Joan's family bible was tired and worn through
its many years of use, it was still particularly grand and would
have been very expensive in its day. Not only did it have an
intricately etched leather cover, but its corners were clad in
metal, and hinges ensured the volume could be tightly secured. The outer edging of its pages were wrapped in gold
leaf enhancing its stunning, albeit tired look.

West Street it seems had been for many generations the
place in which the family belonged. Joan had lived in the West

Street property with her two sisters and parents since birth. Both of her parents had grown up in the street. Grandparents and great grandparents had also lived in an old cottage a little further down the street. Although perhaps not such a practicing Christian family in later years, previous generations had been devoted church goers and records of many family occasions were recorded in their family bible. Many little records of family events such as invitations and birthday cards were contained within the leaves of the old book too. Sadly, some rather more poignant records were there too including a press cutting announcing the loss of a son of the family, killed in action in the first World War.

With the passing of time Joan had found herself alone in the family home. After some persuasion by her daughter, she agreed that downsizing would be an agreeable thing to do. Whilst, given the family history, she would have dearly loved to stay in the vicinity of West Street, unfortunately despite everybody's best effort, no suitable property in the immediate area could be found for her. It was with considerable reluctance and a heavy heart that Joan agreed to relocate to a modern purpose-built apartment in neighbouring Leamington Spa. Moving to a much smaller home brought many challenges including what to take and what should be passed onto family. Joan would not be parted from the precious family bible though. She felt settled in her new environment surprisingly quickly, finding herself less affected by the loss of everyday familiarities in West Street than anticipated. These feelings of comfort were however, soon to be replaced by feelings of fear and unease.

Due to lack of storage space in the new apartment, the precious family bible was now being stored, out of necessity rather than choice, under Joan's bed, the tome neatly wrapped in a dust cover. Early one morning after the move, her daughter received a phone call from her upset mother reporting that she had fallen during the night. While she reassured her panicked daughter that she was OK, Joan herself was more shaken by the mysterious circumstances surrounding her fall. Awaking during the night and with need to use the bathroom, she had tripped over the bible, which for some inexplicable reason, had moved from underneath her bed.

The dust cover had somehow also become completely detached, Joan finding it in the morning on the opposite side of the bedroom. She had spent most of the night after her fall wide awake, trying to make sense of this inexplicable happening. She recounted her movements and actions from earlier in the evening and was sure she had not even entered the room before bedtime. Joan's daughter visited her later that day to check she was OK and ensure that the bible was firmly stored under the bed again, remaining slightly sceptical to her mother's version of events,

Several weeks passed without any reoccurrence of strange activity. After returning home from visiting her daughter in Warwick one evening however, Joan heard a strange sound as she opened her front door. It was the sound of something sliding along the polished wooden flooring in the hallway. At first, she was filled with anxiety at the thought of intruders in the flat. She was instead greeted with a sight that was perhaps even more anxiety inducing. The bible lay at an angle in the middle of the hallway, the dust cover again removed. Although she had never encountered anything remotely like this before, the possibility of some unseen entity at work immediately crossed her mind.

As hard as she tried, she couldn't rationalise the two incidents. She dismissed the possibility of the apartment being haunted as it was very modern. Against her better judgement Joan decided to discuss the issue with her daughter. When she was told of the strange events Jo, rather than disbelieving her upset mother, was this time convinced that something strange was indeed occurring in the apartment. In the hunt for an explanation, she agreed to stay in the apartment with Joan for several nights and together, they set about conducting experiments.

On consecutive nights, they took the bible, placing it in different parts of the apartment each night to see if it triggered any kind of occurrence. The outcome astonished both. Across four nights, the family bible was placed in a different location before they both retired to bed. On three out of four nights, come the morning, the bible had mysteriously moved. On the first night no movement had been made at all. On the second the night book was moved albeit only by a few inches. That alone was enough to unnerved them both, but by dawn after both the third and fourth nights they awoke to find that the bible had been moved to the opposite sides of the rooms in which it had been placed.

Unable to find rational explanation for the occurrences, the bible it seemed was restless, almost as if was seeking sanctuary in a place where it could rest at ease. They agreed that the unusual events had to be as a direct result of Joan's relocation as there had never been any phenomena associated with the book before. Perhaps if the bible was moved back to familiar territory its desire to keep moving might be placated.

Jo was working in a pub in West Street at the time. Whereas Joan had previously been reticent to be parted from the bible, as it would be passed to her daughter in the fullness of time in any event, she agreed to let her daughter take it with her to the Warwick premises to see what consequences, if any, that this would have. The volume was placed on a small refectory table in a back room, and over the course of the next days and weeks, those who had been told the tales of this mysterious moving bible waited. Days and weeks passed, and a peculiar atmosphere began to pervade the little room. However busy and rowdy the pub got there was always an air of peace and tranquility in the bible room as it has now come to be known.

The notion that an object such as a book might be in some way conscious, with thoughts and feelings of its own, is a challenging concept. Many eastern religions such as Buddhism & Jainism recognise sentience in non-humans to varying degrees and theories such as animism and panpsychism present ideas where both mind and matter are inextricably linked, regardless of whether that matter is a creature or an object. Although such theories would have profound implications if ever proved true, there is a big distinction between the concept of an object having a mind and the idea that an object could be conscious and able to act on its own thoughts. The explanation in this instance remains out of reach. The bible has never moved since it has come home to West Street though. It appears that it is once again content, being in its spiritual family home of so many years.

"

One generation shall praise your work to another, and shall declare your mighty acts

(psalm 145:4)

In the aftermath of a fire several years ago at a very old property in West Street, the owners of the listed building found themselves burdened with the daunting task of rectifying the severe damage with the requirement to reconstruct the dwelling to match, as closely as possible, the original structure.

To both theirs and the appointed builder's constant astonishment, attempts to replicate the construction were continually disrupted by unseen intervention. On many occasions reconstruction work would be mysteriously dismantled overnight with no logical explanation apparent. Tools would disappear and construction equipment would fail. Even planting and greenery adjacent to the house that had been replaced, would be found mysteriously uprooted in garden borders.

Throughout Hispanic & Filipino cultures, great superstition often surrounds the alteration or reconstruction of old buildings and the building on historic and culturally significant land. In the Philippines, permission is often sought in the form of offerings or prayers, from the spirits of previous occupants. If this procedure is not adhered to, it is enshrined in folklore that the mischievous mythological dwarf-like spirits, Duende, Nuno Sa Punsa and Kalanget, may all cause great misfortune, interruption, or death to befall on those who fail to seek supernatural acceptance.

After several weeks of bewilderment, frustration and searching for answers, the owners, despite their cynicism and in the absence of any rational explanation, concluded that some kind of paranormal activity may be occurring. The builders agreed to a more meticulous approach at the behest of the desperate owners, willing to compensate them for the additional time and materials needed to accord with the new demands. As each minute section of the rebuild was completed in precise accordance with all historic plans and photographs available, the curious episodes of intervention ceased. After a much-protracted period, almost a year after the originally estimated rebuild time, the property was re-constructed at great additional cost to the homeowners. All works presumably met, not only the exacting requirements of the council but the exacting requirements of the spirits too as, to this day, no further intervention from the ancient surveyors has occurred. Owners of this historic property no doubt hope those same spirits can maintain a watching brief and protect the building from any future fires too.

❧

One of the most attractive building in West Street is a medieval grade ll listed house dating from the 1600s. The timber framed property was constructed in the Wealden style (most found in Sussex and Kent but also built elsewhere). It has what's known as a queen strut roof typical of the period, roughcast tiles with overhanging eaves and casement windows. These houses were very often built for yeoman. Yeomen were often servants in English royal or noble households and, due to the proximity of West Street to Warwick Castle, any yeoman who lived in this property were likely to have had connections to the nobility at the Castle.

Previous owners of this remarkable old house have experienced a considerable amount of paranormal activity over the years, much of it involving one specific character. In more recent years two teenage girls who lived at the property seemed to have drawn the attention of the persistent spectre. Their parents who shared the story, have never seen the spirit that the two girls claimed to have regularly seen.

Sarah, the older of the two girls, experienced her first ghostly encounter one night when she was watching television in her bedroom. At around 10pm, the TV suddenly switched itself off and the misty apparition of a young male dressed in a simple tunic and leggings, appeared from the bedroom wall. She froze as the figure lingered for a few seconds before drifting back through the wall. Regaining her composure but still shaking, she rushed to tell her parents and sister who, quite naturally, were all sceptical of her story.

Several weeks passed without further happening, until one night the younger girl Gemma, was awoken by what she described as the sensation of somebody blowing on her cheek. The encounters captured the imaginations of the two sisters who became absorbed with a want for more experiences. In seeming response to their desires, the activity began to become more persistent.

The second experience for Sarah again occurred when she was alone in her bedroom, this time reading. She felt overwhelmed by a sudden anxiety before, as on the first occasion,

the same misty figure again drifted through the wall. In both parts excited and frightened, she sought to communicate with the spirit, meekly questioning "what do you want?" To her astonishment a response in what she described as a dry whisper came back before the figure again dissipated. "I bid thee come hither". Gemma also had another visitation not dissimilar to her first one. Rather than a blowing on her cheek she was awoken by a tickling sensation on her forehead. This time a smiling figure, mischievously waving a peacock feather, greeted her as she opened her eyes before quickly vanishing.

Being awoken by something unseen became a common occurrence for both sisters, and while this often felt playful and innocuous, one night Sarah's slumbers were disrupted by the feeling of a heavy presence beside her in bed. She awoke to a vision of the phantom moving towards her in a readiness to embrace. Screwing her eyes back shut, in the absence of being able to take any other action Sarah steeled herself, awaiting contact. After whispering the words 'I am Robin' in her ear, the weight lifted from the bed. She opened her eyes to find him gone again.

As months passed, visits from Robin grew less and less until talk between the girls about real boys exceeded the talk of spectral ones. The girls' parents, believe the occurrences were most likely the consequence of active teenage imaginations, the two sisters encouraging one another on to the point of near hysteria. Both girls, now in their early 20s, still maintain however, that their experiences were very real. The current owners of the house have reported that, every now and then, there are signs that a ghost may still be present. Circumstantial evidence in support of Sarah and Gemma's accounts perhaps.

CHAPTER 18

ST JOHNS

During the reign of Henry II in the mid-12th Century, the land on which the impressive St Johns House stands, was given for the establishment of the Hospital of St. John the Baptist and brought into being by the then 3rd Earl of Warwick, William de Beaumont. The Hospital served dual purposes; to help the local poor and ill and to provide casual overnight boarding and food to impoverished travellers such as pilgrims or other wayfarers. The hospital of St John the Baptist was one of two such hospitals in the town of Warwick at the time alongside the Hospital of St

Michael on Saltisford. There was also a cemetery attached to the Hospital site at St Johns.

In 1540, during the Dissolution of the Monasteries by Henry VIII, the property was granted to Anthony Stoughton in reward for his service at the court of four Tudor sovereigns. Stoughton himself never resided at St Johns and by 1610 the site comprised four standing buildings, including a gatehouse topped with crenelations (walls with regular spaces in them through which to shoot arrows). The largest of the three other buildings has crosses at the roof's apex, suggesting its religious use as the site's chapel. Stoughton's grandson: Anthony Stoughton junior, at one time MP for Warwick, inherited the site and commissioned the Jacobean mansion which still stands today, behind large iron gates in neatly tended gardens, In the East Wing of the house there is a door lintel which bears the date 1626 and the initials A.S.

In 1791, the Earl of Warwick rented the house out for public use for the first time, the building coming into use as a school. St John's Academy was founded by William T Fowler and was set up specifically for "Young Gentlemen". Above the porch entrance to the house, the words 'Education' can be seen, a visual reminder of the buildings use during this period. Throughout the life of the school, its attendees often changed. In 1828, the daughters of William Fowler, then running the school, changed it to a school for girls. It was then reverted for boys again in 1845 under a Mr Townsend before once again becoming a girls' school in 1884. The girls school continued to operate from the site until the end of the 19th Century. In the later part of the school's life, as finance became a major issue, the school restricted itself to the lower part of the house, with upper rooms being leased out to local artists and other public figures, with their studios being open for public viewing. The school was eventually declared bankrupt and closed in 1900. For many years the house was open to the public, housing a museum a Victorian kitchen and a school room, where visitors could experience what life would have been like for pupils at St Johns House. Although now closed to the public, the building is still open for use by schools and, can also be hired for other events and ceremonies.

Much history and folklore surround this place and over the years, human remains have been dug up during refurbishment and remodelling works on the House. In the 1830s skeletal remains were unearthed when work was being undertaken in the kitchen garden. In 1987, two workmen digging by St John's Court flats in the area adjacent to Coten End discovered two human skulls. During its time as the Stoughton family residence, much tragedy occurred at the house with the Stoughton daughters Jane & Ann both coming to untimely demises. Jane perished after her clothes caught alight one night whilst stoking the dwindling parlour fire. Ann is said to have died from 'fright' after a burglar entered the property and held her at the point of a blade. The perpetrator fleeing, never to be caught as Ann screamed out violently in fear.

It is claimed that the mansion is the permanent residence of many phantoms and apparitions and, as it is such an active site, it is regularly hired by paranormal investigators and ghost hunters from all over the country. A woman dressed in period clothing has been seen on many occasions standing in front of one of the ground floor windows looking out. In apparent keeping with the known history of the house, the woman is, alarmingly, said to have blackened singed hair with one side of her face appearing as a mass of charred flesh. Those who have witnessed the disturbing vision have also experienced an accompanying revolting scent, like leather being tanned over a flame. The sound of children's laughter, footsteps and cries are also often heard in various rooms throughout the house too. Door banging, and noises from unoccupied rooms and corridors are also regularly heard. The cellar is particularly renowned for ghostly activity. It is said this area is haunted by a very angry malevolent male spirit. Poltergeist activity in the cellar is said to be very common and many, seemingly mostly female, visitors and amateur ghost hunters are known to have beat a hasty retreat from the area, claiming to have been pushed and grabbed by rough, unseen hands.

It is in the gardens of this haunted place that perhaps the most whimsical tale of alleged activity occurs. The path from the car park in St Nicholas Park at the rear of St Johns House leads you along a brook, across a small bridge and through a gate into the gardens of the house. As you enter the gardens you will see, set into a recess in the old sandstone wall, two bronze statues. They are clad in fine Georgian apparel, the lady in a flowing dress, under which she wears a laced bodice, her hair meticulously tied back beneath a bonnet typical of the era. The gentleman wears a tunic and waistcoat together with a pair of high waisted breeches tied at the knee. He also wears a wide brimmed hat. Both are wearing stylish buckled shoes. As with most bronze effigies of their age, time has taken its toll, and the figures are covered in a layer of verdigris (a greenish blue pigment resulting from years of exposure of moisture on the bronze).

There have been many sightings of a female apparition, in period dress gently tapping at the same window from which the badly burnt woman stares. Perhaps the two women are connected in some way. Tiny residues of verdigris have been found left on the exterior glass of the window and, adding further charm to this mysterious story, the tip of the left index finger of the female statue is worn, perhaps through much window tapping over the years. A further incident suggests that both statues may in fact be restless.

After a night of partying and drinking in the town, several late-night revellers passing the gates of St Johns house reported seeing what they thought were kindred spirits in fancy dress, dancing a waltz across the lawns at the front of the house. The assembled group watched through the closed gates of the house, cheering on, and encouraging the playful couple at the centre of this merry scene, until, to their astonishment, arm in arm, the two figures at the centre of the scene suddenly vanished into thin air in front of their onlookers, seemingly tripping the light fantastic together into eternity.

"

The witching hour cometh and 'tis at this time,
from their plinths in the garden, the statues do climb.
The bronze Georgian lovers then dance with delight,
'cross the lawns of St. John's, whilst Warwick
sleeps tight.

Steve Garrison

EPILOGUE

"

'It is certain that human beings possess latent powers of which they are only dimly aware and that these latent powers produce a variety of phenomena from poltergeist activity to 'thought photography' and spontaneous combustion. These 'positive' powers are connected to, but not identical with, the power of precognition and 'seeing' ghosts'

Colin Henry Wilson (English writer of mysticism and the paranormal)

An early 20th century anthropologist determined to expose the 'foolishness' of what he said were primitive beliefs about the existence of ghosts, travelled to a remote African village to simply ask 'do you believe in ghosts?' Upon the question being put to a tribal chief, the man thought carefully. 'I don't know if I believe in them' he replied, 'but I am certainly terrified of them'.

The most recent story I was told came from a local man who had been working alone late one evening in his office in an old building in the centre of Warwick. As he sat at his desk typing on his laptop, he began to feel increasingly uncomfortable. Sweating and shivering, he became consumed by an overwhelming sensation of depression and wondered whether he was experiencing early symptoms of Covid or some other virus. There was another sensation though. It was although something or someone else was in the office with him. While acutely aware to the fact he had been working very long hours and was very tired, he still couldn't shake off this instinctive feeling. Suddenly, a figure emerged in his peripheral vision. Although indistinct he is adamant it was there. It moved as an ordinary person would but was grey and made no sound.

Should we immediately dismiss this story as apocryphal? To do so would imply that this professional man was either lying or had a fantasy prone personality. Maybe stress had created this phantom illusion. Like so many similar stories we will never really know the exact circumstances that conspired to create such an occurrence that evening.

Montague Rhodes James (M R James 1862–1936) is considered by many to be the most prolific English writer of ghost stories, many of which are widely regarded as among the finest in English literature. It is said that he drew inspiration for some of his tales from his own nightmares. His statements about his actual beliefs about ghosts were ambiguous. He wrote 'I answer that I am prepared to consider evidence and accept it if it satisfies me'. During my own research in Warwick, I have met and talked to too many honest and sincere men and women that, even in the absence of any evidence,

I find it impossible to completely disregard the vast majority of supernatural stories that have been relayed to me.

In my own continuing search for answers, I completed a Diploma in Parapsychology and have become a member of the Society for Psychical Research. Yet answers still elude me. Ghosts and other unexplained phenomena remain extraordinary because they continue to evade both proof or absolute refutation by science and pseudoscience. Perhaps the most pragmatic approach to the world of the unexplained might be to try to keep an open mind and acknowledge that even in the modern world of increasingly extraordinary technology, moving alarmingly into advanced artificial intelligence, the answers to most paranormal activity may never be found. It seems to me that, whilst there is still an overwhelming desire among many to resolve the conundrum, an equal number of others wish to preserve the mystery of the unexplained so that we can continue to share and enjoy stories of them.

"

'It is wonderful that five thousand years have now elapsed since the creation of the world, and still it is undecided whether or not there has ever been an instance of the spirit of any person appearing after death. All argument is against it; but all belief is for it.

Samuel Johnson (1709–1784)

ABOUT THE AUTHOR

Steve was born and brought up in Smith Street, a street at the very heart of Warwick Town Centre. A sense of belonging to Warwick has never left Steve and his family history in the Town dates back to the 1600s. Married with three sons and four grandchildren, his late mothers fervent interest in the history and folklore of the Town has inspired similar passions. Steve describes himself as having a curious, questioning and open-minded view of all matters unexplained.

Having undertaken further research and investigation with local people 'Whispers from Warwick 2' is Steve's second book.

I hope you enjoyed this collection of ghost stories and strange tales told by local folk. If you would like to share your own unusual experiences or ghost stories, please feel free to email me at steve.garrison@icloud.com. Who knows…there could be another book waiting to be written.

www.ingramcontent.com/pod-product-compliance
Ingram Content Group UK Ltd.
Pitfield, Milton Keynes, MK11 3LW, UK
UKHW021307180425
5534UKWH00025B/181